CW01655741

WHITE WATER RUNS
AND TOURING RIVERS
OF SOUTH WALES

For Richard Parr and all he meant to me

WHITE WATER RUNS

AND TOURING RIVERS OF SOUTH WALES

A Canoeists Guide

Published in 1990 by Christopher Sladden

ISBN 0 9516147 0 3

Printed by Profile Print Ltd
Unit 3
Sunnyside Industrial Estate
Nelson Drive
Hinckley
Leicestershire LE10 1PJ

Trade enquiries: Chris Sladden,
c/o 43, Hurst Road,
Hinckley
Leics. LE10 1AB

Acknowledgements
I am grateful to the many people who have assisted in this book in some way or another. For those people who have paddled with me, transported me and encouraged me, thank you.

In particular Tim Palmer, Fred Wondre, Punchy Tyler, Nikki Pease and Yramesor Sladden. Thank you also to Malcolm Roberts and Nick Tyler for reading the script, Chris Stent for script presentation, Angelo Conti and Ken Lim for photographs and Huw Evans for information of the Gwili and Tywi. Finally to Mark (I'm a biker now) Crick for encouraging me at times of low ebb and Alfred Blue-Whale I thank you.

Cover photo: the author on the Twrch (low water conditions)

About the Author

Chris Sladden has been living and canoeing in Wales for most of the last eight years. He spent four years at Bangor University, North Wales, where in between the rain picked up a BSC and teaching diploma. He spent a year teaching Chemistry and Outdoor Education before returning to University life in Cardiff to read medicine. He has canoed in Europe, the Nepalese Himalayas and the Peruvian Andes. In 1988 he completed a solo 1,300 mile descent of the river Danube in aid of LATCH, a childrens' Leukaemia appeal.

He is co-author of Italian White Water, and is a British Canoe Union Senior Instructor.

Contents

Introduction

Since moving to Cardiff over three years ago I have been exploring the vast array of paddling waters found here. Desperately hairy (excuse the pun) rivers and bird watching family days out can all be found within an hours drive from Cardiff. We have the rain to fill the rivers too! During the last year, in between lectures and ward rounds and occasionally while the bosses were playing golf, I have been adding the finishing touches to the rivers and notes for this book.

After writing the Italian guide with my pal Tim I am well aware of the barrage of criticism levelled at canoeing guides (and their Authors). One aspect of this criticism that does concern me is the environmental issue. Is it justifiable to open up small streams to hosts of invading paddlers? A couple of runs I have kept to myself because locals have asked me to do so. However, most people I have met enjoy watching others 'doing their thing': especially so when they are polite, shut gates and use sensible access and egress points. Small groups on small rivers will also help (- refer to Access section). The environment is there to enjoy but also to respect and I have tried to encourage this. I hope that you will not use the information in this book to spoil the rights and pleasures of others.

Whilst being recirculated in a weir stopper during a solo trip (after all friends with more floatation probably wouldn't have got out as easily) it did cross my mind as to why I was there. When I eventually hauled myself onto the bank I began to remember. I had experienced heightened emotions of every sort during paddling. I had visited new peoples, new places and formed lasting friendships and these are important. I had learnt much and would learn from this. Paddling has kept me relatively sane over the last few years, especially whilst playing at learning to be a Doctor.

This book tells you where to go, where it is prudent not to go and when to go, but the doing is far better than the telling. I hope you can join me.

Chris Sladden 1990

River Canoeing and Using this Guide

Canoeing is growing in popularity, and paddlers are constantly seeking new water to run. Here in South Wales are a host of rivers ranging from gentle, lazy streams to raging torrents.

Many of the rivers are fairly comprehensively described here although certain stretches have not been included. This is because, for one reason or another, I have not got around to paddling them myself. Unless otherwise stated, the information contained in this guide is based entirely on personal experience.

DISCLAIMER

The descriptions are based on how it was at time of paddling. I make no claim that the rivers are safe at all conditions and for every canoeist. The decision to paddle is yours alone. I must disclaim any responsibility for any injury caused to persons or property in this potentially dangerous sport.

CHANGING RIVERS

The rivers contained in this guide, like any other rivers change, sometimes dramatically with time. Man, ever responsible, causes many of these changes in the form of weirs, canalization, pipes, bridges and neck high barbed wire fences.

Nature too plays an important part in the shape of fallen trees and floods which change the river bed.

It is also possible that misunderstandings between myself and readers may arise. The message is clear, use the guide, but to avoid misinterpretation with unpleasant consequences ALWAYS INSPECT BEFORE PADDLING.

WATER LEVELS

River levels are fundamental in the decision whether to paddle or not. The decision not to paddle may be because the river is too low or too high.

Common sense must prevail on this one. Too low and the canoe may need to be repaired, or environmental issues may be stirred. Usually (not always) the river will be a less serious proposition when too low.

Conversely if the river is too high the grades and therefore seriousness may change out of all proportion from those described here.

Most of these rivers require a steady rainfall to bring them up to typical winter day levels on which these gradings are based. Fortunately, South Wales has more than its fair share of rain. It is difficult to give clear advice on river levels. Gauges do exist on many of these rivers but more often than not they are half way down the run and difficult to inspect. Makeshift

gauges, such as number of rocks covered, are personal and open to misunderstandings, and I have made a point of not using these. On some rivers, the Rhondda for example, it is easy to give hints by saying the boat should float without bumping and scraping.
Grades of river do change, usually increasing with a rising water level. Where possible I have tried to indicate the extent of the change in grade by using a dual grading system. For example the Pen y Cae Falls on the Tawe are graded IV when normal and V when high and are thus graded IV-V. (Incidentally, a grade VI can be given for when the river is abnormally high).

The message is clear - Inspect everything before paddling.

ACCESS

A contentious issue is access. It must be stated from the outset that the words access and egress used in this guide, are no evidence whatsoever of any right to get on or off a river. What is written here should not be taken as advice to trespass. If you decide to paddle on non-access agreement rivers then either access and egress using public rights of way or ask the landowner for permission.

There are access agreements for rivers such as the Usk and for details of these phone the regional or local Access Officer (details from Welsh Canoeing Association or the BCU).

On many of these rivers I have found friendliness from both fishermen and locals, especially in hitching lifts whilst dripping wet. Returned consideration from canoeists, for example by politeness and using gates and paths, can only enhance this. Sport for all should be the message for all concerned.

THIS FRAGILE ENVIRONMENT

One of the worst cases of lack of sensitivity and common sense by canoeists I ever saw was a university club roaring up to the Fairy Glen with two minibus loads of paddlers. These small rivers were never meant to take such numbers. Some of the South Wales streams are big enough for three or four paddlers, but no more in a team. Common sense will prevail, I hope.

Descriptions, Characteristics and Gradings

The rivers in this guide are described in a roughly geographically clockwise order. Each includes an approximately scaled map to help with the descriptions. Figures and references from the appropriate O.S maps are used for access and egress points.

The descriptions are not meant as an eddy by eddy, rock to rock analysis. They are meant to show suitable access and egress, notable falls, potential hazards, portage and an overall indication of what the river is like. I only hint at the best way to run a rapid, and that must be subjective to some degree. The real fun is left for you to discover.

There are five characteristics of the rivers in this guide that are of fundamental importance to the paddler. The first is predominantly associated with rivers high up in the mountains. This is the occurrence of flash floods which may alter the grade of a river out of all proportion. I have personally seen the Twrch Gorge become an uninviting prospect after an hour of heavy rain on top of already spate conditions.

The second characteristic is the presence of waterfalls on many of the mountain streams. It could be disastrous to run one of these by mistake.

Very importantly, many of these rivers pass through heavily wooded areas and a tree or branch may block the canoeist's path. Due to the nature of some of these rivers it is quite impossible to stop on some rapids if, for example, a tree blocked the way. The seriousness of a rapid may be increased out of all proportion to the grade.

A fourth hazard is the presence of weirs or sluices on many South Wales rivers. Especially in high water these may produce very dangerous stoppers and tow-backs.

A fifth danger on some of these rivers is the presence of low pipes that cross the river and tunnels down which the river disappears. Tunnels are very exciting but there is no real way of knowing if they are clear, of for example a tree, at time of paddling - unless you paddle them!

GRADING RAPIDS

Grading rivers is a difficult task. As I wrote in "Italian White Water", to my mind two main problems exist. Firstly, there is no universal grading system that every paddler accepts, and secondly, even if there were people would still grade rivers differently. No matter how objective one tries to be, subjective grades still creep in. It is easy to grade a river as hard if one follows a poor line and takes a bashing on a usually easy run. "It's a hard IV" "No, it's an easy V" type arguments are familiar to most.

Downgrading of rapids is also a tendency of paddlers, especially by the paragons of the sport.

Grades III, IV, V and VI are usually where the discrepancies exist (and also the serious consequences). The presence of a weir or tunnel on a fast grade II section may make it dangerous.
I have tried to comment on this in the text rather than by adding a specific dangerous or serious grade on top of the six tiered system used. Grades IV, V and VI are serious according to the definitions used. It seems somewhat inappropriate to add a serious factor to a grade VI run. Protection can at times make such a rapid safer and I have tried to comment on this. If a river is continuous at a particular grade it will usually make it more serious but not more technically difficult than a single rapid. I have tried to comment on this.

I have tried to grade these rivers as it would appear to someone with experience but running them for the first time. I have used the same grading system as in "Italian White Water" trying to give examples of well known British runs for comparisons. To my mind the most important thing is that readers should have as clear a picture as possible as to what I mean by a particular grade.

DEFINITIONS

Grade I - Easy: Moving water with the odd disturbances in the shape of small regular waves and slight meanders.

Grade II - Moderate: The water is faster and rapids are more frequent; rocks, waves and small stoppers are found but always with an obvious channel.

Grade III - Taxing: The pace quickens with fairly big waves, and stoppers which are quite capable of holding a boat firmly. Rapids are much more continuous and although the route is still fairly obvious it is necessary to be able to manoeuvre the kayak well.

Examples

i) River Trywern, graveyard and slalom section, North Wales.
ii) Upper River Leven (high water) Lake District.
iii) Holme Pierrepont (high release).

Grade IV - Difficult: Long stretches of heavy rapids and falls with irregular waves and often powerful holding stoppers. The route is not obvious from the water and bank inspection is usually necessary. A mistake or swim could be serious.

Examples

i) Town Falls, River Dee, Wales.
ii) The middle Ogwen (usual high water conditions), North Wales.
iii) Cobden's Falls, River Llugwy, North Wales.

Grade V - Extremely Difficult: Longer rapids, larger drops with very big waves, dangerous stoppers and rocks to negotiate. This is a challenge to any canoeist. Although never absent in the other grades, in grade V substantial danger is always a possibility. Continual inspection and/or protection is often necessary.

Examples

i) The Aberglaslyn Gorge (just off flood), North Wales.
ii) The Fairy Glen, River Conwy, North Wales.
iii) The Middle Ogwen (in full flood), North Wales.
iv) The Wallowbarrow Gorge, River Duddon, Lake District.

Grade VI - Limit of Navigation: A line down exists - just. Luck may often be the factor concerned. There is always a real risk to life. Very favourable conditions, water levels and protection may make rapids of this grade feasible. Most of the time, however, they are too dangerous to canoe.

WATERFALLS

Many waterfalls are runnable only when the rest of a river is too low to contemplate. Perhaps, under these conditions, many could be described as bottle, neck and back testers! It usually isn't feasible to run falls such as these when the rest of the river is worth doing. It is for this reason I tend to describe them as waterfalls, best portaged, rather than grade VI rapids, and not to challenge someone to prove me wrong!

PORTAGES

Uncanoeable sections, for whatever reasons, are marked as portages 'X'.

WEIRS

Dangerous weirs are marked as definite portages, whilst comments are made on those requiring inspection. Unusual spate water can make normally safe weirs dangerous. Complacency towards weirs is always risky. I almost paid more than I was prepared to whilst soloing a South Wales river because of this. The message is clear - If In Doubt Portage.

Maps and Key to Symbols

The large scale sketch maps on pages 14 and 15 have been included to show the approximate location of rivers.

Hand drawn maps have been included for each river. They are not drawn to exact scale as they are intended to give quick visual information to the canoeist. Used in conjunction with the text they provide information on access, egress, nearby roads, major falls and portages. It should be noted that they are not drawn to show all landmarks, such as every bridge. Some rivers, for example the Rhondda, have in excess of twenty bridges crossing them. To show or indeed describe all of these would be meaningless. Rivers flow in the direction of access to egress.

Obviously, a large scale map, preferably a 1:50 000 Ordnance Survey would be advantageous to the visiting canoeist not familiar with the Area. The name and number of the relevant O.S. map have been given in the river descriptions.

Six figure grid references have been given for access, egress and certain public houses.

Key to Symbols Used

Symbol	**Description**
	Portage - uncanoeable
	Weir/Sluice
	River
	Bridge
	Access
	Egress
	Gorge
	Road
	B - road or track
	Direction of river flow
	Tunnel
PH	Public House

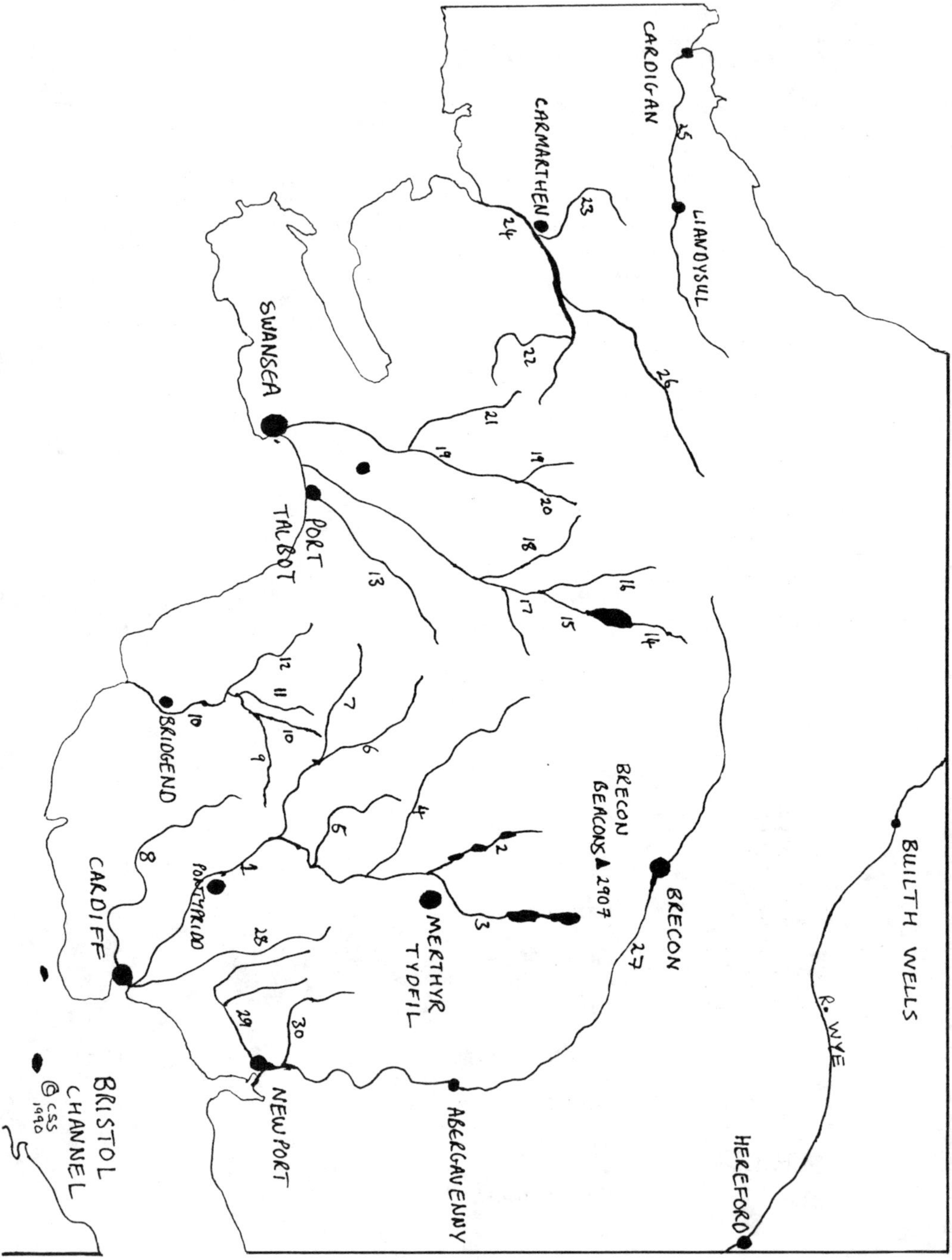
CARDIGAN
CARMARTHEN
LLANDYSUL
SWANSEA
PORT TALBOT
BRIDGEND
CARDIFF
PONTYPRIDD
MERTHYR TYDFIL
BRECON BEACONS ▲ 2907
BRECON
BUILTH WELLS
R. WYE
HEREFORD
ABERGAVENNY
NEWPORT
BRISTOL CHANNEL
© CSS 1990

Location Map

Number	River
1	Taff
2	Taff Fawr
3	Taff Fechan
4	Cynon
5	Nant Clydach
6	Rhondda Fach
7	Rhondda Fawr
8	Ely
9	Ogwr Fach
10	Ogwr Fawr
11	Garw
12	Llynfi
13	Afan
14	Nant y Gwair
15	Dringarth
16	Llia
17	Mellte
18	Nedd Fechan
19	Tawe
20	Nant Tywynni
21	Twrch
22	Sawdde
23	Gwili
24	Tywi
25	Teifi
26	Cothi
27	Usk
28	Rhymney
29	Ebbw
30	Lwyd

AFON TAFF

Maps: Cardiff, Newport and surrounding area No. 171
Vale of Glamorgan and Rhondda area No. 170
Length: 39 Km
Grade: Sections of I-II and II-III, 1 rapid V plus weirs.
Access: A470 and A470(T) Cardiff to Merthyr roads.

Notes One unpleasant grade IV-V fall which reaches V+ in spate. Many of the weirs need portaging.

General Introduction

If pollution is ever solved then the Taff will lose its major stigma and become a great touring river. Although at first a seemingly gentle Welsh river, a few surprises undoubtedly exist for the paddler to find. Just occasionally, due to its massive catchment area, the Taff has a correspondingly massive flood. In these conditions it is far better to go and paddle one of the tributaries, described elsewhere in the book, than to risk a hammering in one of the many weirs.

ABERFAN TO PONTYPRIDD 18 Km Grade II-III (1 fall V)

This section is usually good for up to a few days after heavy rain. Take the B4285 turning to Aberfan off the old A470. Where the road crosses the river it is possible to put in below a two stepped weir. GR072002. The first mile through the town is best passed quickly after which an excellent wooded section is reached. At good river levels the rapids are an entertaining grade II-III with numerous playspots. This is a superb area for kingfishers!

Care needs to be taken when approaching Quaker's Yard where a nasty grade V rapid awaits. This can be easily inspected during the drive up. An unpleasant plug of rock awaits at chest height in the first of the two drops on the right. Nasty in any conditions, it becomes a serious V+ in spate. Portage right.

Below Quaker's Yard are two weirs. Both are obvious from the river. The first is best portaged because of shallow landings and debris. The second can be run down the large central tongue although high flows can iron this out. Inspect! The Cynon and Nant Clydach entering from the right swell the river. This section is excellent for playing. Two stoppers, formed by pipes crossing the river bed, provide some amusement. There is one rapid of note just before an old bridge on the outskirts of Pontypridd. Best taken on the left to avoid upstream pointing rock slabs. Egress is on a small road, river left. GR074906

AFON TAFF - section 1

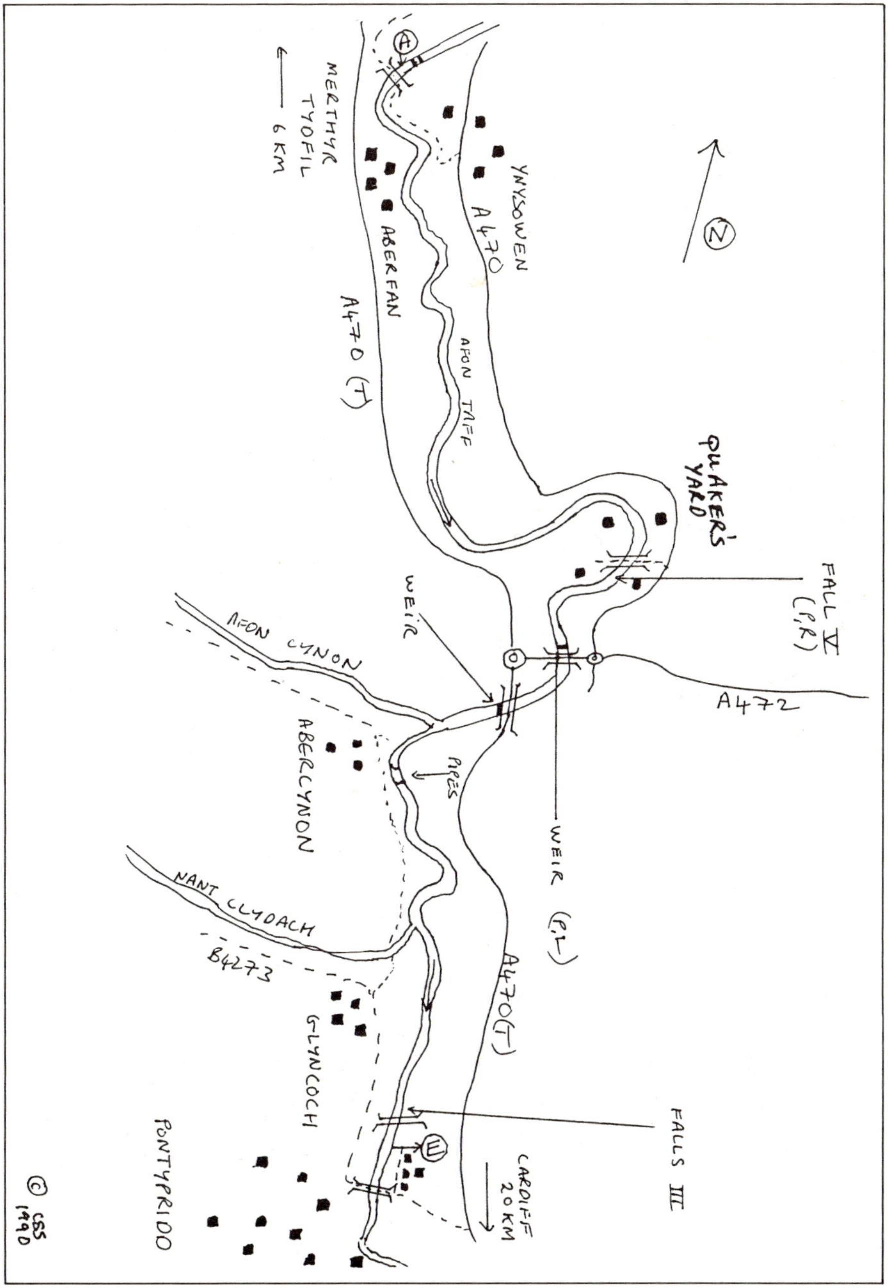

PONTYPRIDD TO CARDIFF 21 Km Grade I-II and Weirs

Access at the above egress point for this pleasant paddle to Cardiff. There are five weirs on this section and three are best portaged. The first, about 2 km from the start is obvious from the river and is best portaged. The second is below the main road bridge to Treforest. This is a large vertical horseshoe affair and is best portaged with some scrambling on the right.

The third is at Radyr just after the M4 road bridge. This can be shot with care at normal river levels. The fourth at Llandaff rowing club is another large angled affair, shootable with care. A good egress point is by Tal y Bont Halls of Residence GR170783 just off North Road, Cardiff. Far better to watch salmon jumping the weir below than to shoot it. The purist may wish to paddle to the sea and egress up mud banks in Grangetown. On route you will pass the Castle (well worth a visit) and on International Day hear the roar from the Arm's Park.

Inspecting the Twrch in flood.
Photo: Angelo Conti photo library

AFON TAFF - section 2

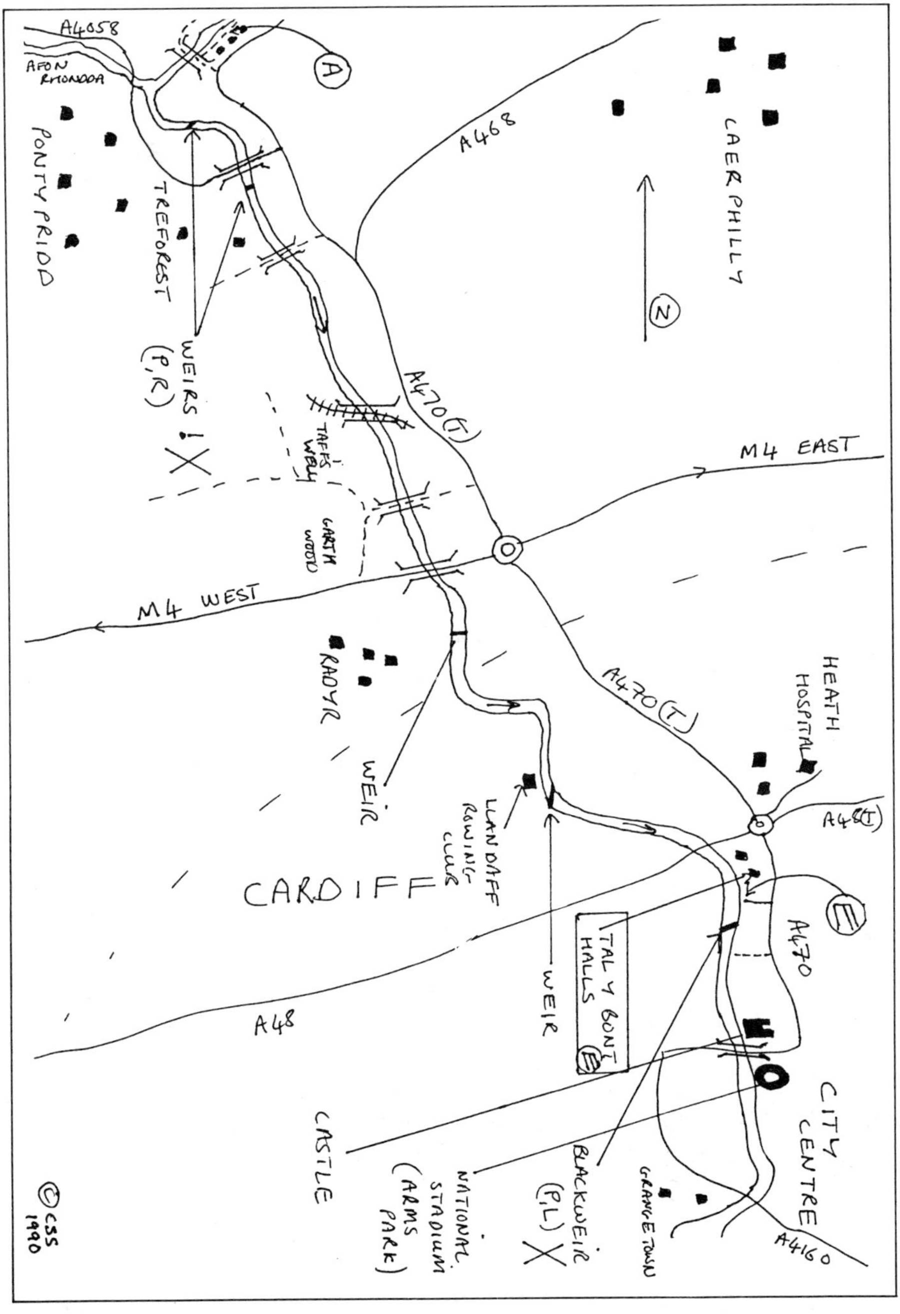

THE TAFF TRIBUTARIES

AFON TAFF FAWR

Map: Brecon Beacons No. 160
Length: 2 and 3 Km
Grade: II - III
Access: A470 (T) Merthyr to Brecon Road

Notes Fences may need portaging

General Introduction

Two fast stretches of stream paddling.

BEACONS RESERVOIR TO CANTREF RESERVOIR 2 Km Grade III

Put on below the A4059, GR989182 road bridge for a fast spate run to the next reservoir where it is best to egress. Care needs to be taken because of trees and wires crossing the river.

CANTREF TO FOREST CENTRE 3 Km Grade II - III

Take the drive down to the waterworks and put on just above a small weir GR999152. A huge overflow shoots water in just above. The first rapid is a good grade III with the only problem being overhanging branches. At time of writing there were 3 fences to negotiate between this and the next reservoir. A good egress point is at the bridge crossing the river just above the reservoir GR005132. The weir below is best portaged.

AFON TAFF FECHAN

Map: Brecon Beacons No. 160
Length: 7 Km
Grade: III - IV, 1 Fall IV - V
Access: A470 (T) Merthyr to Brecon Road

Notes Undercuts in the various gorges make this a serious run for the grade.

General Introduction

An exciting run over steps and through shoots and narrow gorges.

PONTSTICILL TO MERTHYR 6 Km Grade III - IV (1 Fall IV-V)

When the river is up it is possible to put in at the little bridge across the river at GR060107. This is reached by turning right off the A470 just past the Brynmawr turning. Carry on up to Pontsticill where there is a right hand turn in the village leading to the bridge. Grade II - III water rushing between bushes and eddying behind cars (thrown in the river) is your first taste of the Taf Fechan. Many, therefore, will prefer to put in above or below Pont Sarn. Just above here an old viaduct which is often used for abseiling spans the river. A grade V mini gorge and following fifteen foot drop is found at the road bridge. The shoot is more straight forward than it looks but several undercuts make it potentially dangerous. The water eases off before picking up to pass through several rocky gorges on its way to Merthyr. Undercuts make swimming potentially dangerous and there were several trees jammed in the river at time of writing. Some may require portaging. Egress is at the A470 road bridge - a bit of a scramble up on the right. GR038077

Wild Water - South Wales style. Photo: Chris Sladden

AFON TAFF FAWR & TAFF FECHAN

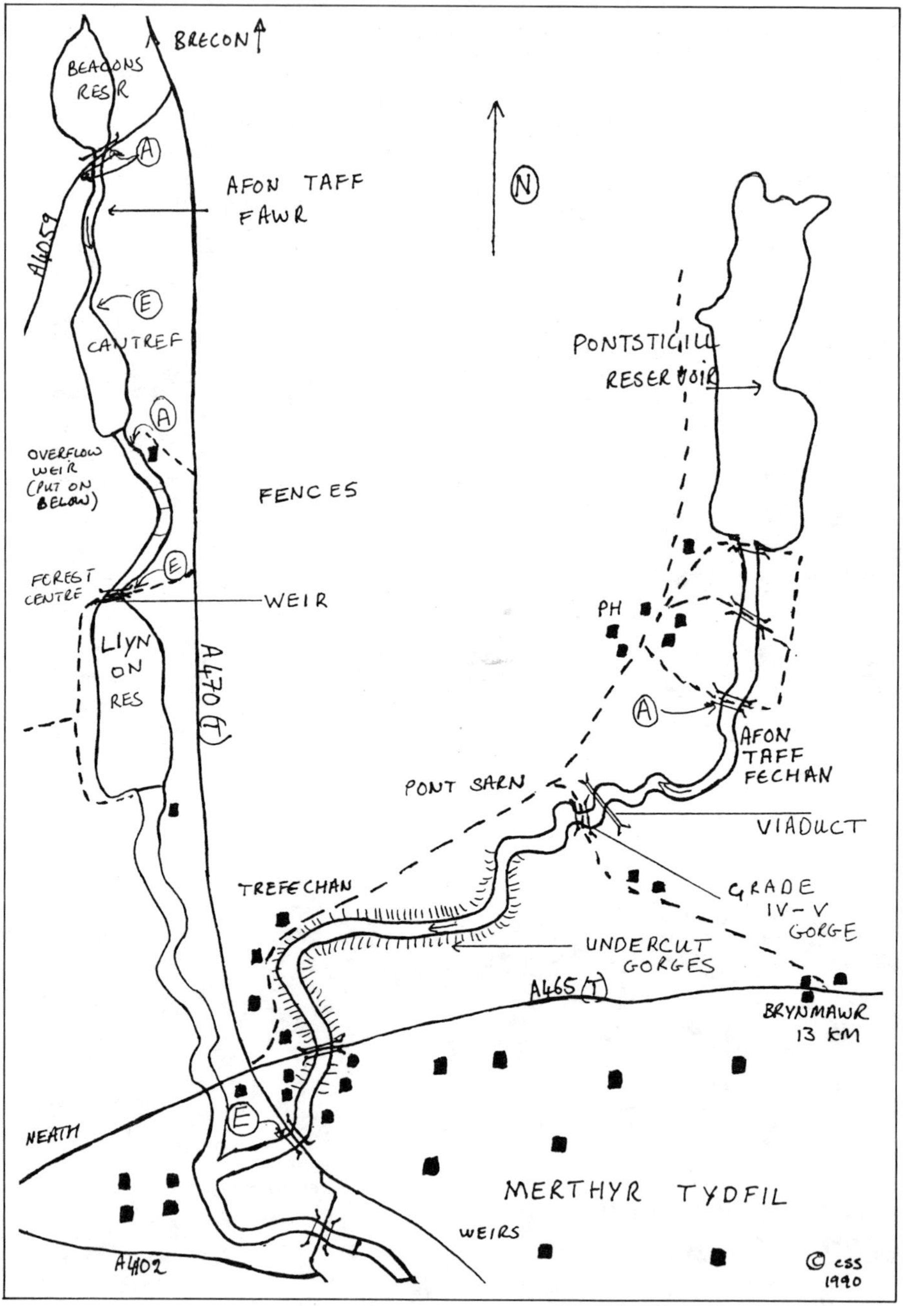

AFON CYNON

Map: Vale of Glamorgan and Rhondda Area No. 170.
Length: 8 Km
Grade: II
Access: A4059 Abercynon to Aberdare Road
Public House: The Maltsters - Pontypridd

Notes 3 Weirs and trees

General Introduction

This is an odd one to recommend, because of the valley through which it flows. However, the Taff into which it flows and the last couple of km of the Cynon provide entertainment.

MOUNTAIN ASH TO TAFF CONFLUENCE 8 Km Grade II

Put on, if you dare, in this incredibly used Welsh valley at a small footbridge that crosses the river upstream of Mountain Ash. This is found just before the large industrial workings spurting forth flames 2 km upstream of the town. GR037997

There are three weirs on the river. The first, below a railway bridge in Mountain Ash is difficult to inspect or portage. A climb up a crumbly bank on the right some 100 m before is best. Although broken it forms a strong stopper.

The second is obvious from the fiver a few km downstream and is broken in nature. The third as the river nears the Taff usually consists not of a stopper but a superb standing wave. It is just below a footbridge. It is best to continue into the Taff and egress a couple of km downstream where the river nears the road. GR080933

NANT CLYDACH

Map: Vale of Glamorgan and Rhondda Area No. 170
Length: 8 Km
Grade: II - III Plus one gorge of IV
Access: B4273 Pontypridd to Ynysybwl road
Public House: Ynysybwl Inn by portage on upper section

Notes 2 definite portages. 1 Fence, 1 low bridge. A tight gorge in the lower section.

General Introduction

I love this river and the surprises it holds. It's only big enough for a group of about 3 people and the locals are friendly so please don't abuse this!

PORTHCELYN BRIDGE TO TAFF CONFLUENCE 8 Km Grade II - III(IV)

The Nant Clydach needs to be in spate to run. Get in at the road bridge crossing the stream at GR048967 (Ynysybwl to Miskin road). An alternative for the adventurous is to run the Y Ffrwd some 2 km lower downstream. This enters the Clydach via some fast big drops.

If the river is brown and over the banks at the get in then the run will be a hectic grade III. Slightly lower, the river is more manageable at II - III. Continual grade II takes the paddler through a tunnelled bridge. Shortly after the bridge, a fence needs to be portaged. Trees and 2 more sets of wires after this need to be treated with caution. A fording bridge at the Ynysybwl Inn needs portaging (unless in big spate when the water goes over!) GR055951 The river, now bigger in volume with the entry of the Y Ffrwd passes through Ynysybwl where it rushes down a 70 m tunnel hewn out of the rock. The roar gets louder as the paddler bounces out of control and in the dark through this and over the small weir at the other end. This is best taken on the left to avoid metalwork in the centre. It should be stressed that although it is tremendous sport to run this tunnel it is difficult to know if any debris has been left inside from the last storm! Portage if in doubt.

A grade III slot and a small weir follow. The weir buries you in the stopper below. A pipe crossing the river, thankfully over a quiet pool needs to be sculled under or portaged. As the river nears the road and Glyncoch is approached there is an excellent grade IV gorge. The first fall is quite technical and the drop before the following road bridge has a tree in it. A permanent resident for the last three years it needs to be treated with caution.

There is a tree blocking the next railway bridge. Portage, although in high water you won't even know it's there! The rapids continue until a final rush just before the following small road bridge. Beware metalwork debris in this rapid. Egress onto the road. GR080928

AFON CYNON & NANT CLYDACH

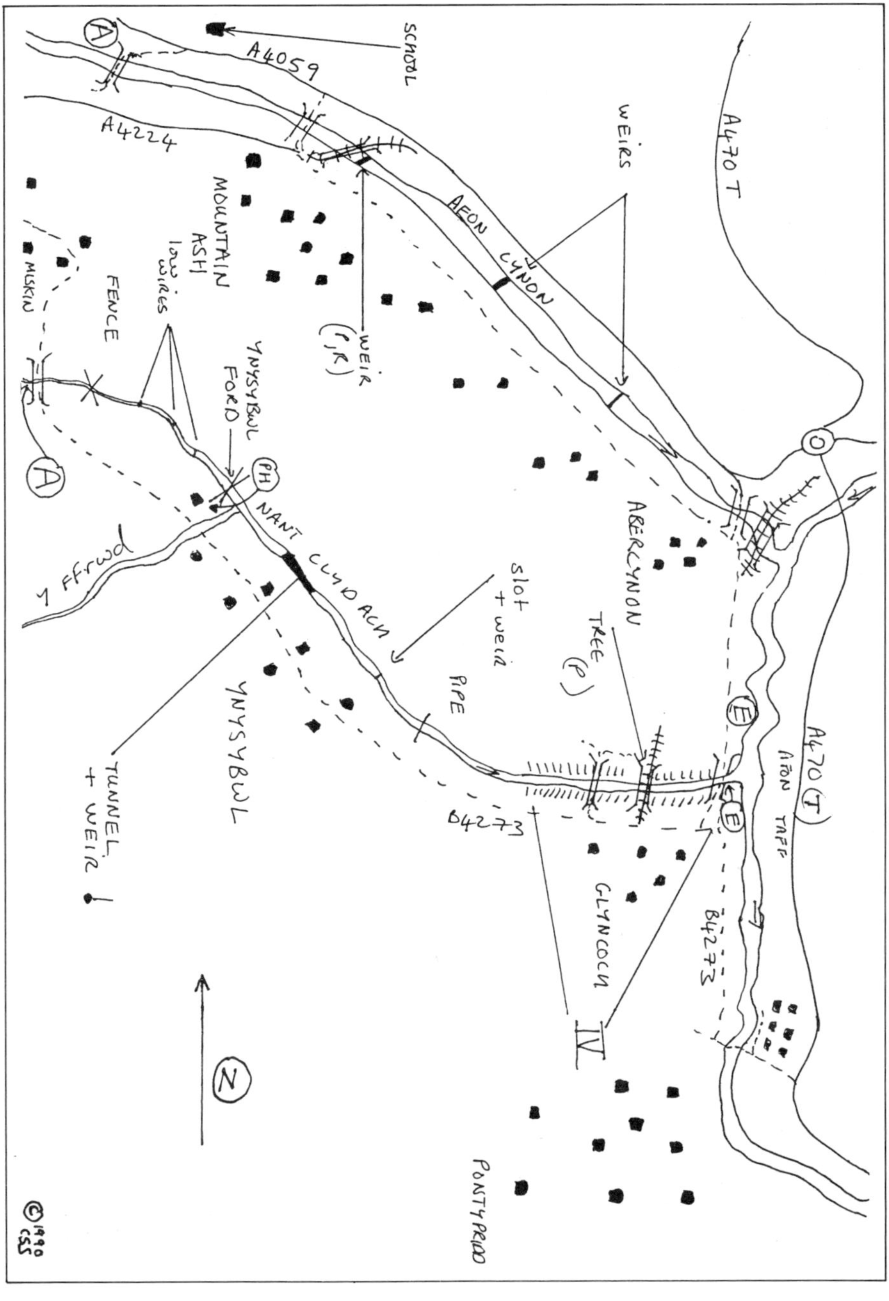

AFON RHONDDA FACH

Map: Vale of Glamorgan and Rhondda Area No. 170
Length: 5 Km
Grade: II One rapid grade III
Access: B4277 Porth to Maerdy road
Public House: Maltsters, Pontypridd.

Notes Two pipes crossing the river - one a definite portage.

General Introduction

The Rhondda Fach would be a beautiful river if the rubbish adorning its banks were removed. There is plenty of wildlife however, which seems to put up with this.

PONTYGWAITH TO PORTH 5 Km Grade II (III)

Start the run at the main road bridge crossing the river in Pontygwaith GR012939. There is a convenient parking space just by the bridge where you can also put in. A few hundred metres down and a pipe needs to be either squeezed under or portaged depending on river height. Grade II water follows, passing quickly down a short tunnel and over a few weir steps towards Porth. Here a pipe spans the river and needs to be portaged. Just before the confluence with the Rhondda Fawr some man made steps under a road bridge give a grade III rapid.

Exciting enough at its grade, the trip is best finished by carrying on down to Hopkinstown, described under the Rhondda Fawr section.

AFON RHONDDA FAWR

Map: Vale of Glamorgan and Rhondda Area No. 170
Length: 26 Km
Grade: II - III plus two rapids grade III - IV
Access: A4058 Pontypridd to Treherbert Road
Public House: Marquis of Bute, Treherbert.

Notes Three low pipes - one portage.

General Introduction

Canoeing through the valleys has a charm of its own, and although strange at first, there is an abundance of wildlife including kingfishers.

BLAENCWM TO PORTH 20 Km Grade II - III

Turn off the A4058 in Treherbert towards Blaencwm and pass through the village of Tynewydd where you turn left under a bridge. Access can be had on the Nant Y Gwair just above the confluence with the Rhondda

GR928991. There should be ample water to float the canoe on this small stream. Start off on fast grade II with sharp eddies for those new to this type of paddling. Soon a small weir with measuring gauge is reached. This should read at least 3 to make the run worthwhile. At 9 or 10 the grade will be III. The gauge is visible just behind the bus stop GR935985.

There are so many bridges on this river that one loses count very quickly which makes it pointless describing them! However, they do provide alternative access and egress points. Care should be taken at the first of the pipes crossing the river some 4 km from the start. Portage right if the water is high.

The urban is forced back by the rural as the river passes through woods before Llwynypia. The next problem is a small weir below which another pipe spans at chest height. It can just be squeezed under on the left. Below the large road bridge in Tonypandy is a pipe which needs to be portaged left or right. Approach with care! Bouncy water including a broken weir step takes the paddler to the confluence with the Rhondda Fach.

PORTH TO HOPKINSTOWN 5 Km Grade III - IV

This section acts as a surprising finish to the upper stretches. The river doubles in volume after the confluence and shortly after the first main road bridge in Porth is a weir step with a surprisingly strong stopper.

About 2 km below Porth in between the two crossings of the A4058 a railway bridge spans the river. The river here surges over a series of partially man made, partially natural steps. The middle channel through the bridge is the best entry to avoid concrete structures on the left. It is best to inspect from the pipe in the right arch, for some of the ledges in high water carry large stoppers - best avoided. Some good waves are found under the next road bridge after which the river eases off until just before Hopkinstown. Here, under a small bridge the river is compressed to give a short grade III - (IV) rapid. Egress is river left just before the town GR061904.

AFON RHONDDA FACH & FAWR

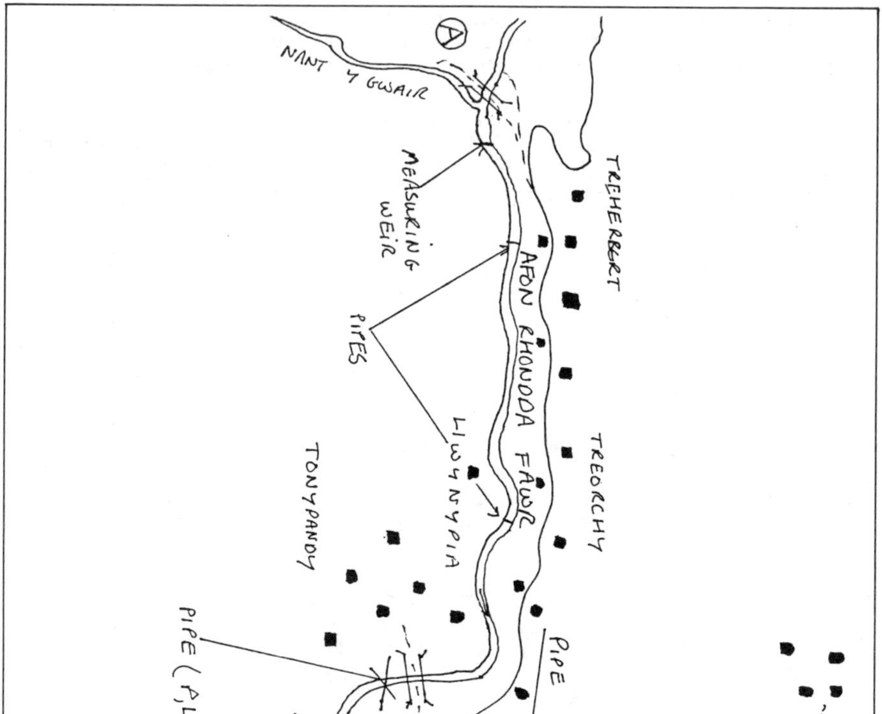

AFON ELY

Map: Glamorgan and Rhondda Area No. 170
Cardiff, Newport and Surrounding Area No. 171
Grade: II
Length: 30 Km
Access: M4 Junction 34 A4119 to Tonyrefail

Notes Low trees require care

General Description

A gentle relaxing touring river.

DYFFRYN TO CARDIFF 30 Km Grade II

Start the run at the small bridge that crosses the river on the edge of Llantrisant Forest GR023852. From here the river bubbles along under bridges, over small weir steps and around trees towards the M4, under which it passes. From here it meanders in large slow loops with deep crusty banks towards Peterston Super Ely. An excellent place, this, to see wildlife.

After Peterston the river straightens out and some steering is required, especially in high water, to avoid overhanging trees. A small measuring weir near the Welsh Folk Museum and a couple of broken weir steps are the only other disturbances before Cardiff. Egress may be made at the small bridge in St. Fagans GR119770 or at the next major road bridge at Ely, Cardiff GR146768. (A weir after this is difficult to portage should you fancy a trip to the sea - I haven't done this).

AFON ELY

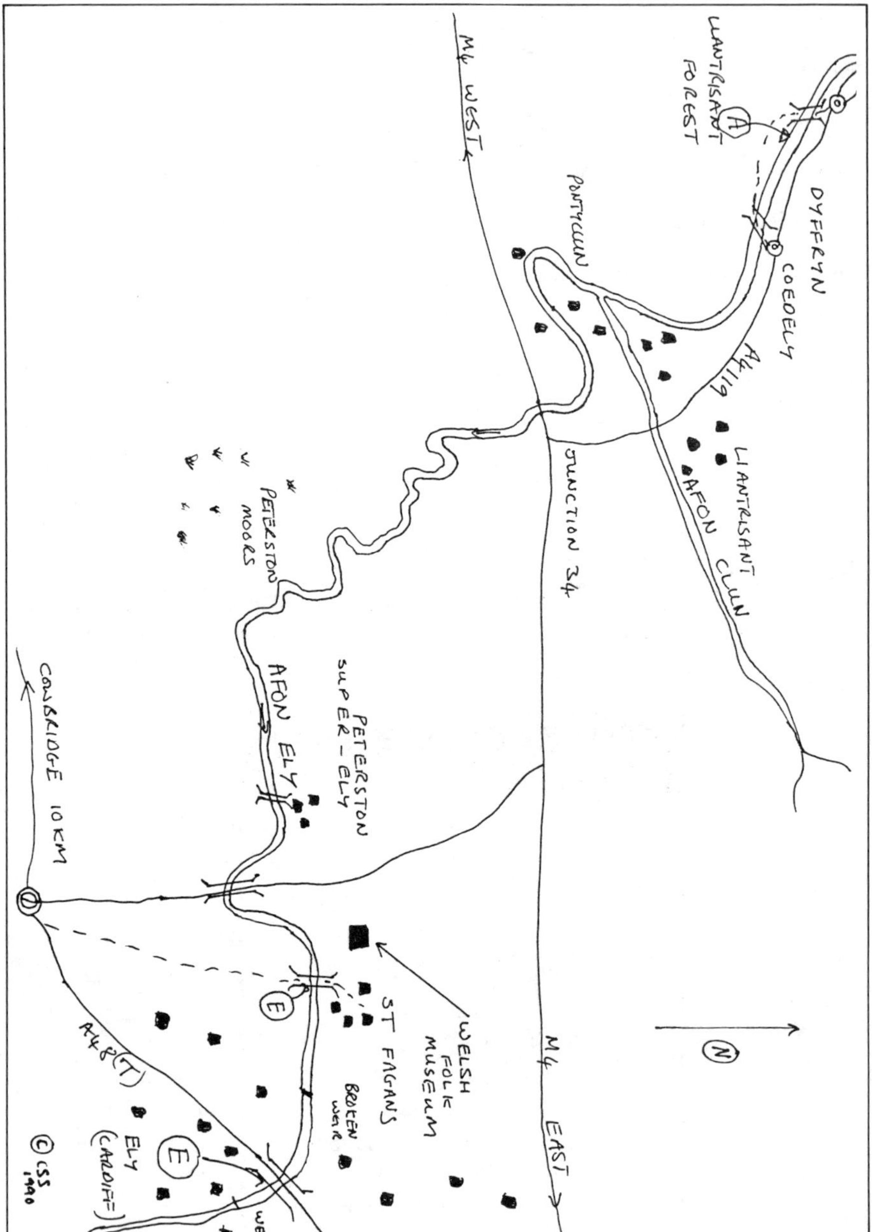
M4 WEST
LLANTRISANT FOREST
A
PONTYCLUN
DYFFRYN
COEDELY
A4119
LLANTRISANT
AFON CLUN
JUNCTION 34
PETERSTON MOORS
PETERSTON SUPER-ELY
AFON ELY
COWBRIDGE 10 KM
E
ST FAGANS
WELSH FOLK MUSEUM
BROKEN WEIR
M4 EAST
N
A48(T)
E
ELY (CARDIFF)
WEIR
© CSS 1990

THE OGMORE VALLEY

AFON OGWR FACH

Map: Vale of Glamorgan and Rhondda Area No. 170
Length: 7 Km
Grade: III
Access: A4093 Blackmill to Tonyrefail road.
Public House: Tyler Arms

Notes Three fences need to be portaged. Trees may require portaging.

General Introduction

This is the smallest tributary (within reason) of the valley and one many would laugh at. However when full to the brim it gives a tremendous run albeit serious at the grade due to trees and fences. A new type of break-out called "grabbing the banks" is needed on this type of river!

EVANSTOWN TO BLACKMILL 7 Km Grade III

Turn off the A4093 on the B4564 to Evanstown. Access may be had where the road crosses the river by putting on below the tunnel through which the river rages GR979893. This stream wants to be over the banks for an exciting run. A hanging fence a short way down needs to be portaged. Two further fences between the next farm and road bridge need portaging (asking permission useful here!) Just after these fences is an excellent set of weir steps to bounce through to just past the road bridge.

The river continues under an old railway bridge and accompanying farm bridge. Soon after these, two huge concrete tunnel pieces thrown into the river need to be carefully steered around. From here to the Ogwr Fawr confluence the only problem is trees depending on recent storm damage. At the time of writing one of these needed portaging.

Egress just before the main road bridge at the confluence onto the left bank GR933867. Better still, continue down the Ogwr Fawr where you will be in for a bouncy ride at this water level!

AFON OGWR FAWR

Map: Vale of Glamorgan and Rhondda Area No. 170
Length: 20 Km
Grade: II - III
Access: A4061 Junction 36 of M4 to Ogmore Vale
Public House: Tyler Arms GR873892

Notes One pipe after the confluence of all the rivers requires portaging.

General Introduction

A good run. If you can turn a blind eye (and maybe other senses) to the sewage works at Merthyr Mawr then an excellent trip will be had.

OGMORE VALE TO MERTHYR MAWR 20 Km Grade II - III

When the water is up it is possible to start the run up in Ogmore Vale. Take a small road, first on the right, on entering the town from the M4 side. This runs through football pitches to a small bridge across the stream GR934896. If the water is too high a railway bridge 100 m downstream needs to be portaged. There are three fences slung from railway bridges and one other that need to be portaged or dodged. Take care.

After the confluence things improve dramatically and indeed you may wish to put in here. Between here and the Garw confluence is an excellent series of steps which in big water have powerful waves to negotiate. After the Garw confluence and around a left hand bend is a metal banked section with a double stepped weir at the bottom end. This forms boxed-in stoppers that need to be treated with respect if the water is high! Portage if in doubt. If the water is 1 m below the top of the gauge then the river is well up although it can be run at much lower levels.

After the confluence with the Llynfi and just before passing the motorway is a pipe spanning the river that needs portaging. This is covered in extremely big water but to swim would be potentially very dangerous! Bouncy waves and closed-in banks take the paddler through Bridgend to a weir with a strong stopper in high water. A slipway on the right and low banks on the left allow escape if needed. The weir is fairly obvious from the river although difficult to find as you drive hopelessly lost around Bridgend. Far better to buy some cream buns rather than trying to find it and inspect from the river. Extremely pleasant touring water takes the paddler under ancient stone bridges to Merthyr Mawr. Egress by a footbridge into a car park on the right GR883774 or further down the Estuary. The dunes at Merthyr Mawr and the castle are well worth a wander.

AFON OGWR FACH & FAWR

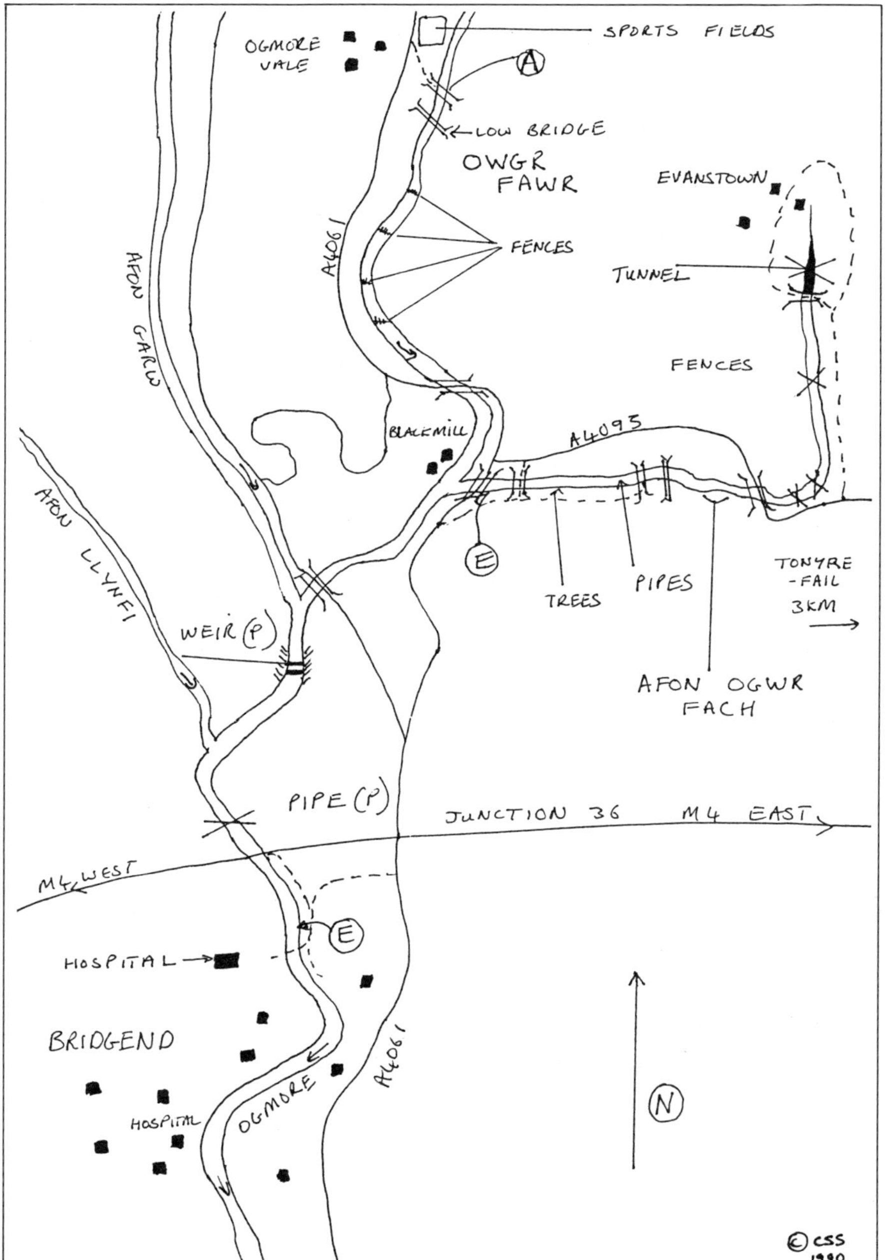

AFON OGWR / OGMORE

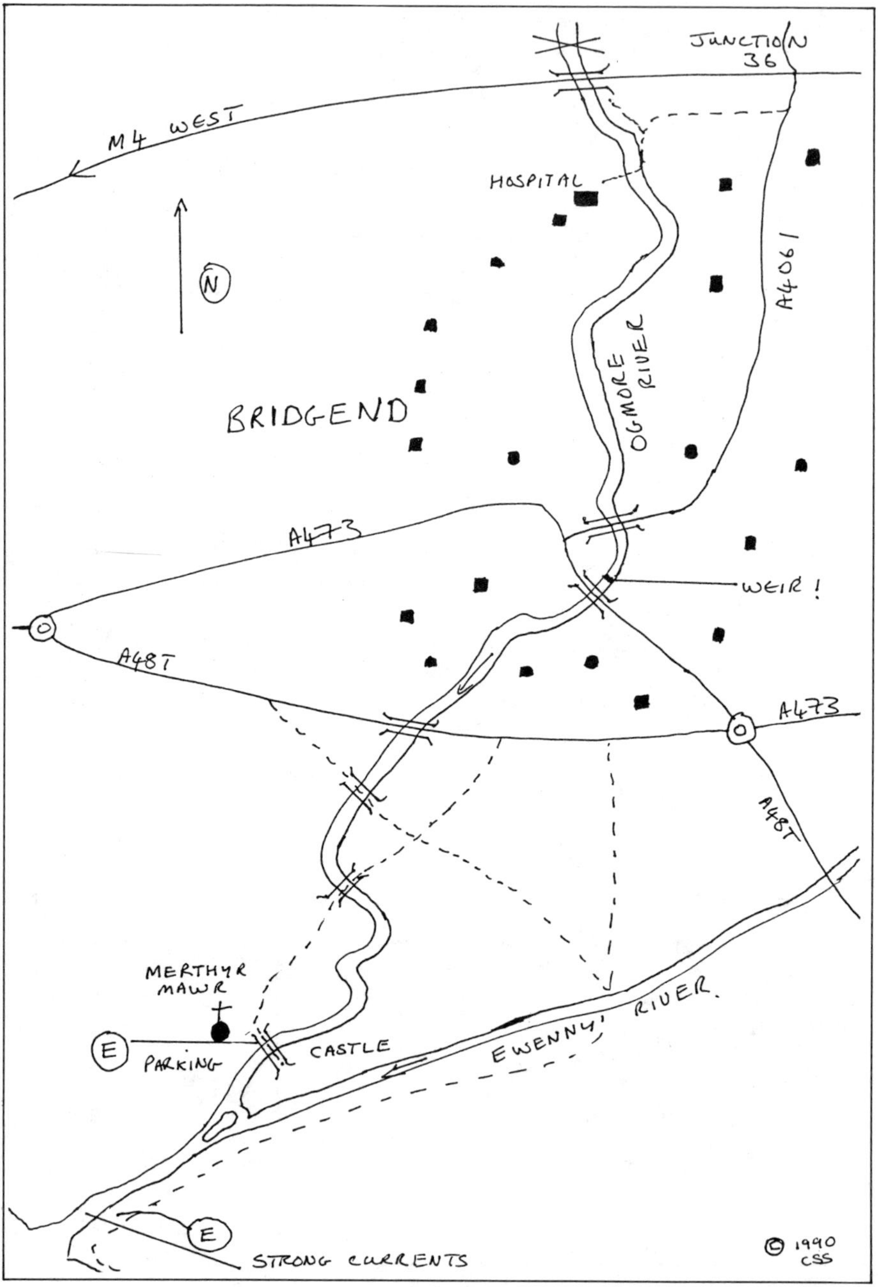

AFON GARW

Map: Vale of Glamorgan and Rhondda Area No. 170
Length: 9 Km
Grade: II
Access: A4064 Junction 36, M4 to Pontycymmer road.
Public House: Braich y Cymmer

Notes Several portages around low fences and trees.

General Introduction

An easy, pretty river teeming with bird life but with the odd surprise in store.

BRAICH Y CYMMER TO OGMORE CONFLUENCE 9 Km Grade II

Start the run at the railway crossing just by the Braich y Cymmer public house GR905898. This fast running stream takes the paddler into a wooded valley where trees may be a problem. Barb wire spans the river twice before the next road bridge. This is passable with care. Just after the next road bridge the river bends sharply to the left and the paddler must crash through overhanging bushes (in Llangeinor). The river bends back to the right and a fence needs to be portaged river right. Further on, just before a railway bridge, another fence requires portaging on the right. The next two low bridges need squeezing under at normal water levels. Wooded banks and, therefore, trees will always keep the paddler on his toes as Brynmenyn is approached. Rhododendron bushes begin to mark journeys end and a wooden adventure playground on the right makes for an amusing respite. Only one fallen tree over which the river pours remains. Egress at the main road bridge in Brynmenyn on river left GR907848 or continue down the Ogmore.

AFON LLYNFI

Map: Vale of Glamorgan and Rhondda Area No. 170
Length: 9 Km (16 Km)
Grade: II
Access: A4063 Bridgend to Maesteg Road
Public House: Tyler's Arms GR873892

Notes One pipe just after the confluence requires portaging. A few small weirs are present.

General Introduction

An easy touring river, good for groups.

PONT RHYD Y CYFF TO BRIDGEND 9 Km Grade II

It is possible in high water and entertaining enough in its own way to start the trip above Maesteg adding a further 7 km to the run. A small bridge in Nantyffyllon GR853930 marks the start. Break outs behind (or even into) shopping trolleys, a couple of short tunnels and a passage between debris caught on a pipe are amusing if not taxing. A more reasonable place to start is by the Tyler's Arms pub at Pont Rhyd y Cyff GR873892. The river flows gently with trees on bends being the only problem. A weir found on a left 90 degree bend just by the obvious buildings on the right bank provides entertainment for those needing it. Further on is a small measuring weir.

The confluence with the Ogmore makes the river more bouncy but no more difficult. Continue down portaging the pipe described in the Ogwr Fawr section. Egress may be made by the bridges near the hospital GR903822 or up the steep banks to the nearby small roads. Alternatively carry on down the Ogmore.

AFON GARW & LLYNFI

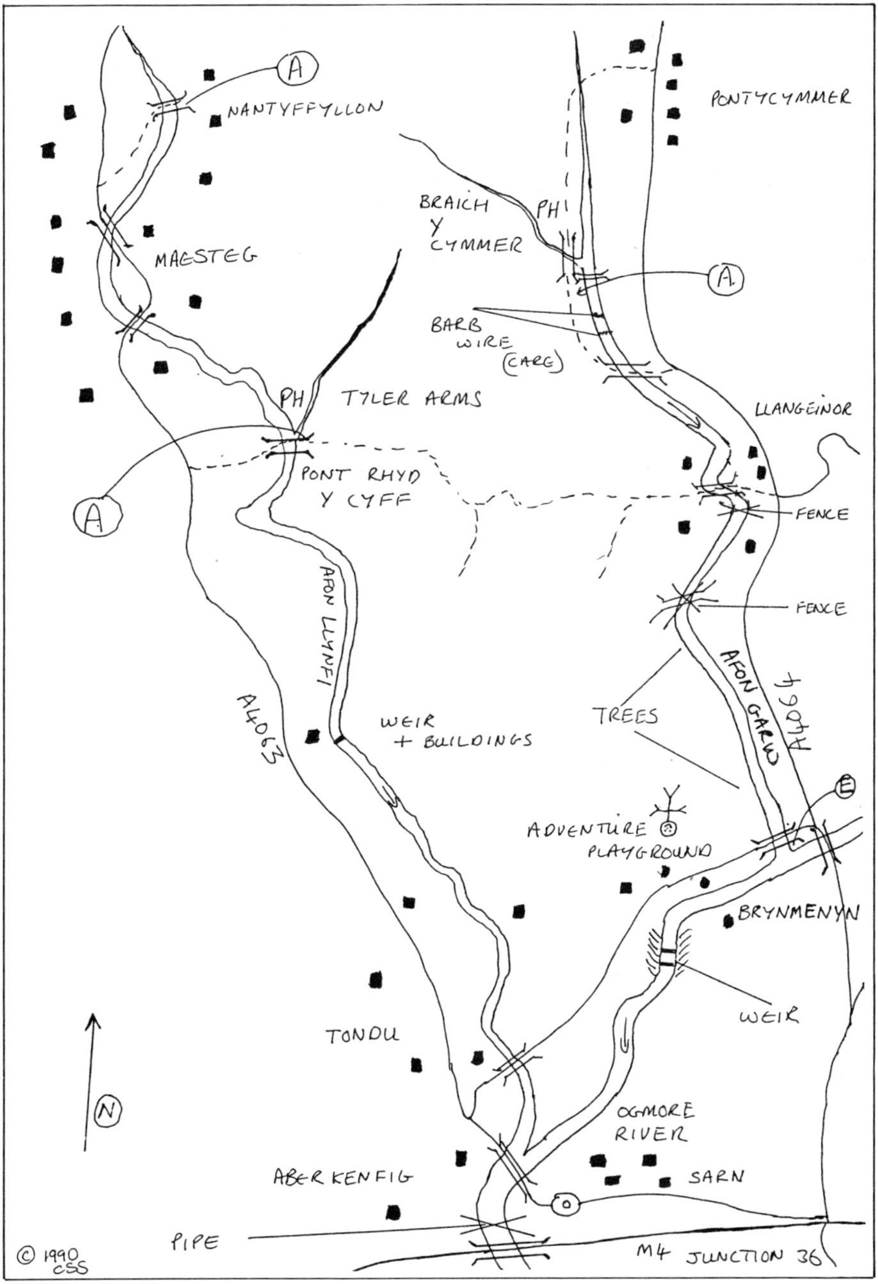

AFON AFAN

Map: Vale of Glamorgan and Rhondda area No. 170
Length: 15 Km
Grade: III
Access: A4107 Port Talbot to Treorchy road

Notes One tree which is a portage on the upper section. Two pipes below Cymmer require great care.

General Introduction

An excellent fast run especially in high flows.

CYMMER TO PONTRHYDYFEN 11 Km Grade III

In high water the run down from the bridge in Blaengwynfi to Cymmer is an excellent grade III. Apparently one tree needs to be portaged although I personally haven't run this section.

Put in from the left bank of the Afon Corrwg, a short distance up the Cymmer to Glyncorrwg road GR862966. (At high levels it is possible to put in higher up). Once on the Afan the river is fast and bouncy and fun. However, beware, for above and below an obvious football pitch are two pipes spanning the river. Although it is possible to pass these obstructions at certain water levels, there is always a danger of being strained underneath if mistakes are made. In flood these pipes are covered. Portage if in any doubt.

From here down through the Afon Argoed Park is an excellent run at a good grade III level. Egress in Pontrhydyfen just below the road bridge GR795942. A weir just below this will back end the unwary so take care.

AFON AFAN

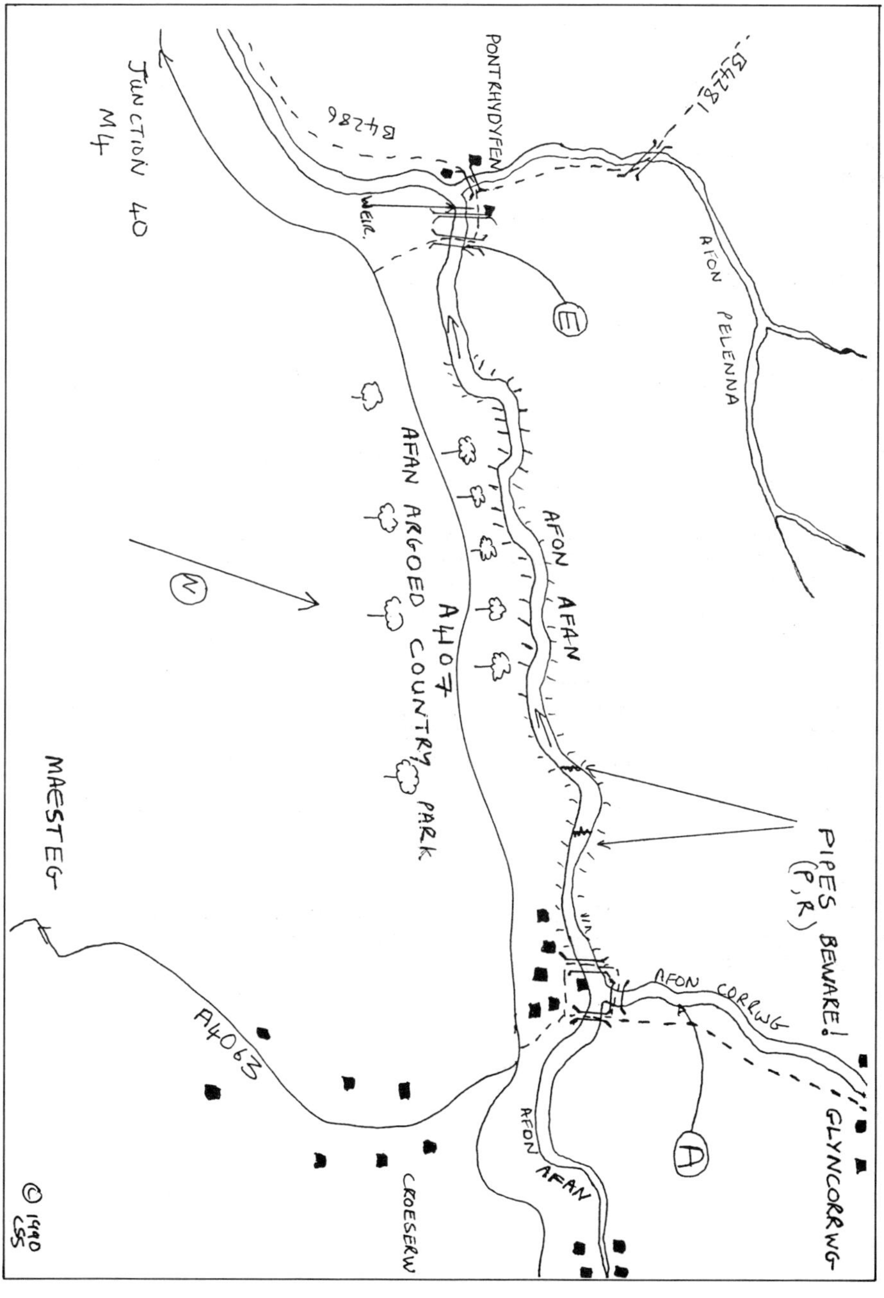

PONTRHYDYFEN
B4286
B4281
JUNCTION 40
M4
WEIR
E
AFON PELENNA
AFON AFAN
A4107
AFAN ARGOED COUNTRY PARK
N
MAESTEG
PIPES (P,R) BEWARE!
AFON CORRWG
A4063
AFON AFAN
A
GLYNCORRWG
CROESERW
© 1990 CSS

FFOREST FAWR BASIN

NANT Y GWAIR

Map: Brecon Beacons
Length: 2.5 Km
Grade: IV (1 fall V)
Access: Ystradfellte to Sennybridge road
Public House: New Inn, Ystradfellte

General Introduction

An expedition in the making.

RHOS DRINGARTH TO YSTRADFELLTE RESERVOIR 2.5 Km Grade IV

It is only possible to recommend this short stretch to the highly adventurous. The walk in with the boat takes about one and a half hours and it needs to be heavily raining at the time. It is possible to walk in from the old Roman Road skirting around Fan Dringarth GR935204. Alternatively and probably better is to carry on from the walk in to the Afon Dringarth, described below. This is via the footpath on river right of the Afon Dringarth starting just before the confluence with the Lliw GR937144.

All these rivers are only big enough for three or four paddlers so please use common sense. The family on the farm through which the footpath runs are true gems so please treat them as such! They are quite happy with small groups paddling the rivers and allow landing on the right hand banks.

Start the run as high up as the boat will float. In spate the paddling is grade IV with one fall of V just before the confluence with the Nant Y Gaseg.

A strainer prevents the paddler entering the reservoir which is probably a prudent move. You could either run back up for more goes down or walk along to the Afon Dringarth for another brilliant run.

AFON DRINGARTH

Map: Brecon Beacons
Length: 4 Km
Grade: III - IV One fall V
Access: Ystradfellte to Sennybridge road
Public House: New Inn, Ystradfellte

Put on (as above) via the right bank well below the reservoir. In big spate the river is a serious grade IV but at normal high levels (bouncy grade II water at confluence with Afon Llia) it is a good grade III. About a km down, there is a sloping fall with a fence stretched across the bottom of it. At grade III levels this can just about be sneaked under.

The banks close in and a large vertical fall blocks the river. This grade V fall can be run middle to left or via the left hand chicken shoot. (Always depth check falls like this!) In flood it produces an enormous stopper! Below this 2 fences need to be portaged on the right. Otherwise enjoy a beautiful river in tremendous surroundings. Egress at start of walk in. One word of note: don't leave boats lying about, they have a habit of being pinched. If they do, ring the police who from experience, will know the culprits! A moral lies hidden here somewhere!

AFON LLIA

Map: Brecon Beacons
Length: 3 Km
Grade: III - IV
Access: Ystradfellte to Sennybridge road
Public House: New Inn, Ystradfellte

Notes Fences need to be avoided. One fall is portaged.

General Introduction

A fast mountain stream requiring caution because of low trees and fences. One Fall is best portaged. Paddled with the Dringarth, it makes an excellent day out.

GR928165 TO AFON MELLTE Grade III - IV

Start the run at a parking place just off the Sennybridge road. Put on below a fence crossing the river. When the river is in flood the paddler quickly passes down through a forested area. Inspection for trees is required. About half way down on a left hand bend is a major 18 ft vertical drop into a shallow pool. This has been shot but is best portaged. Some of the drops below reach grade IV. Care is required as the confluence is reached because of trees across the river. One required portaging at the time of writing.

Nant y Gwair. Photo: Ken

NANT Y GWAIR, AFON DRINGARTH & AFON LLIA

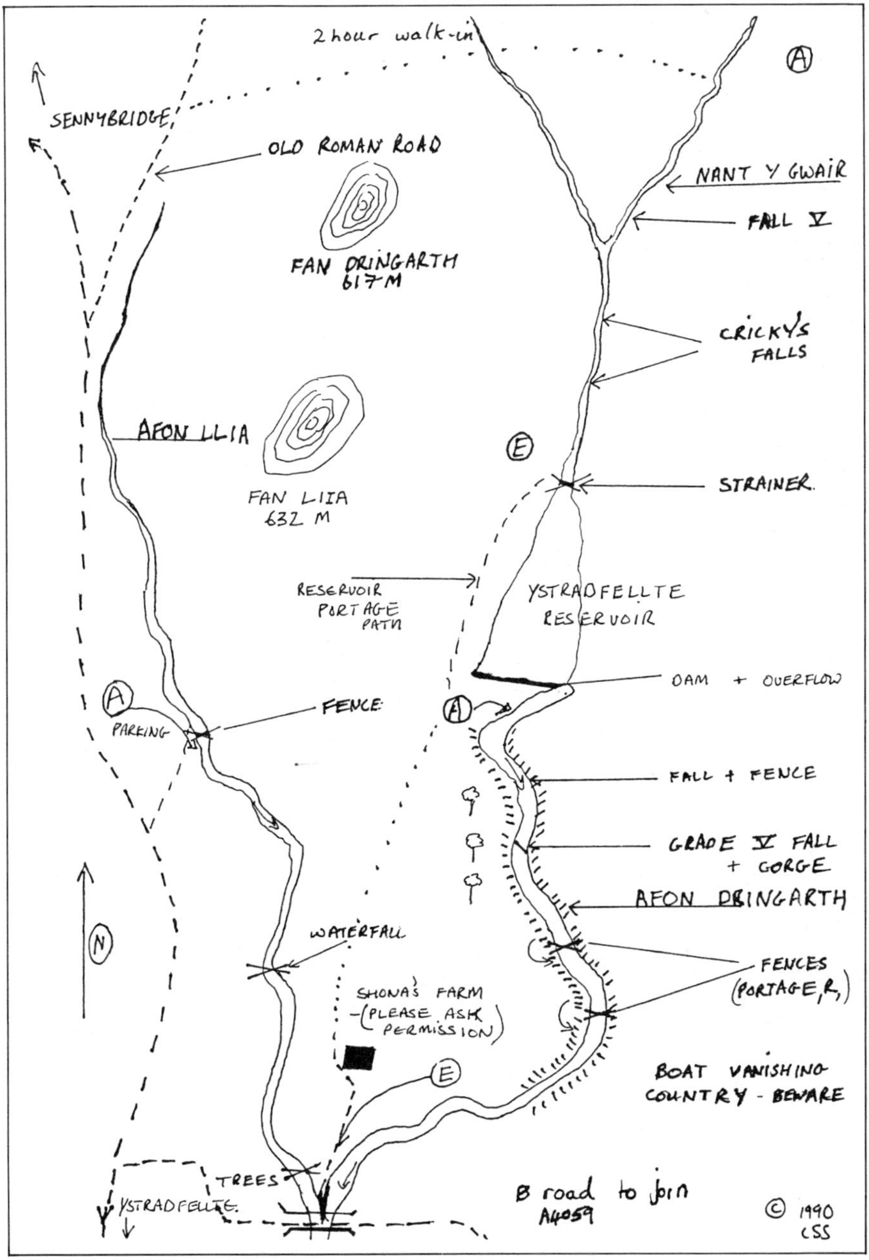

AFON MELLTE

Map: Brecon Beacons No. 160
Length: 6 Km
Grade: IV - V
Access: Pontneddfechan to Ystradfellte via A465(T)
Public House: New Inn, Ystradfellte

Notes Several waterfalls need to be portaged.

General Introduction

An excellent river, albeit serious in places. Recommended for people paddling at this level. The portages are a small price to pay for the isolation of this gorge.

PORTH YR OGOF CAVES TO PONTNEDDFECHAN 6Km Grade IV - V

Access to this superb river from the Porth Yr Ogof caves car park reached by a small turning off the Pontneddfechan to Ystradfellte road GR928124. Put in on the pool below the cave exit. The water should be high enough for a line down the first grade II to be had without much scraping. Easy water takes the paddler to a new footbridge after which a grade IV series of steps rushes directly over a huge drop. This is Sgwd Llun Gwyn waterfall which although it has been shot is definitely a prudent portage on the right.

Easy water takes the paddler to the next portage a short distance on. Again Sgwd Isaf Clun Gwyn has been shot but is a portage by the prudent. Put on below for the squirts, drops and squeezes downstream. Some short distance on is the Sgwd y Pannwr waterfall. This large diagonally running vertical drop is more feasible to run than the others but still constitutes a good V at high levels. Inspect before running to leave yourself good time to portage up the steep right hand bank. Grade III water takes the paddler down to some more grade IV - V sloping rocky drops just before the Hepste confluence.

The section after this is an excellent run with narrow squeezes, shoots and squirts to negotiate through mini gorges. Care should be taken as a few of these drops had trees jammed in them at time of writing. A couple of the very narrow shoots can form big tow backs with no room for paddle strokes and so inspection is required before running. Down this section is a man made vertical weir. This is a strange thing to find in a gorge such as this despite being made out of natural rock. If the water is very high you may wish to portage as the stopper has been known to give a severe thrashing on such occasions. Some way after another footbridge is another weir with some large blocks at the bottom of the second step. A good egress point is at the gunpowder works road bridge in Pontneddfechan GR911079.

AFON NEDD FECHAN

Map: Brecon Beacons No. 160
Length: 3.5 Km
Grade: III - IV (V when high)
Access: Pontneddfechan to Ystradfellte
Public House: Angel Inn

Notes Two waterfalls require portaging

General Introduction

A fine river in beautiful surroundings.

PONT MELIN FACH TO PONTNEDDFECHAN 3.5 Km Grade III - IV

Take the first turn off left from the steep Pontneddfechan to Ystradfellte road. This crosses the river at Pont Melin Fach where there is a convenient car park by the river GR908105. The paddler sets off on easy water in a beautifully wooded gorge. Some few hundred metres on is a 3 m double drop. There should be ample water over this if the run is to be worthwhile. A short distance further around a right hand bend is the first portage. This, 20 foot vertical drop (known as Wondre's Wonder) is too shallow to run!

Inspect the next few hundred m as the second portage occurs soon after. This is another large vertical drop and a definite carry.

Using throw ropes allows the adventurer to put in right below the plunge pool. The next section of drops is excellent sport with one triple drop being particularly tricky to negotiate without pinning on. A short exciting section leads to the final drop. This is a left to right diagonal fall which has a tree which is a pretty well permanent fixture on the left hand side of the stopper. Inspect and be aware that this is covered at high water.

The river is joined by the Afon Pyrddin before making its way at grade II - III to Pontneddfechan. It is best to egress at the stone bridge GR901077 and straight into the conveniently placed public house.

AFON MELLTE & AFON NEDD FECHAN

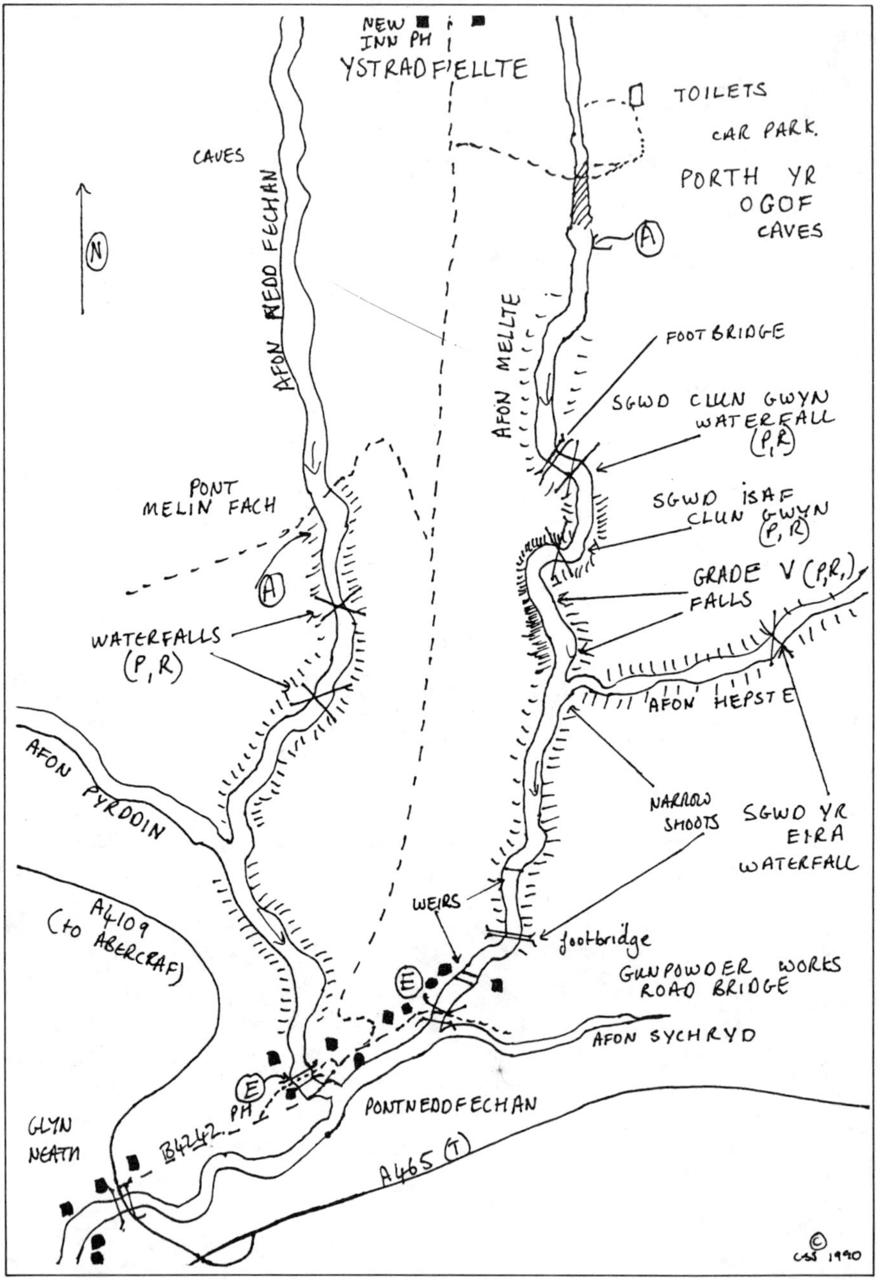

AFON TAWE

Map: Brecon Beacons No. 160
Length: 14 Km
Grade: Section of III, IV, V, (VI in spate).
Access: A4067 Abercraf to Sennybridge road

Notes One fall on the upper Tawe needs portaging due to a jammed tree. There are other possible portages depending on water level.

General Introduction

A brilliant river which can give a superb grade V+ run in high water. I'm well into double figures of running this stretch and I'll be back: Wonderful.

THE UPPER TAWE MAEN MAWR TO GLYNTAWE 7 Km Grade IV-V-VI

Depending on water levels this will be grade IV, V or VI and even well known paddlers have walked off from here!

Take the small road to Trecastle which branches off the A4069 just past Glyntawe. This follows the river and access may be had where the stream comes very close to the road above a series of respectable drops GR852213. (In very high water it is quite possible to run the drops from another 2 km higher up). As an indication if you scrape at the access point the gorge below will be IV, if rocks are covered it will be V and if the drops by the access start backlooping it will be grade VI, a very serious undertaking! It is wise to inspect the gorge beforehand!

Exciting water takes the paddler away from the road and over a series of large slabs IV - V. Soon after, the rocks close in and a fantastic narrow gorge is entered. The drops are fast and furious. A fifteen foot vertical drop on a right hand bend requires some thought. Some of the following drops are undercut, and one stopper on a narrowing, just above a vertical 10 ft drop almost invariably backloops a boat at high water levels!

A footbridge appears with the river dropping out of sight just beyond. It is essential to inspect this next hairy section as 150 m further on a tree blocks the bottom of a blind drop. A portage is essential and it is very difficult to stop in high flows.

The water eases off to an apparently gentle grade IV before the banks open and the best is over. Carry on down past the Nant Tywynni confluence to the bridge at Glyntawe where egress can be made. Continue down the lower section if you have adrenalin left.

GLYNTAWE TO ABERCRAF 7 Km Grade IV - V (V when high)

Access as above, GR846168, for this second superb section. The grade can easily vary by 2 at different water levels. Grade II III water takes the adventurer through the Craig y Nos country park to the bridge at Rhongyr Isaf GR845145. If the water is flowing through the trees right over the banks on route then the run below this bridge is a serious undertaking. Egress if in doubt.

An excellent grade IV run through large waves and holes takes the paddler down to the Pen y Cae Bridge. In full spate this section rises to a serious grade V with some enormous almost river wide stoppers forming.

There are some large falls over sloping slabs just below the Pen y Cae bridge which become a very serious undertaking in high water. Enormous stoppers are a very frightening prospect V (VI occasionally!). If in any doubt portage left.

Some hundreds of metres further on is a large natural vertical fall. The route must be left for you to decide - right is the safest but avoid an undercut slot left of centre! The river rushes through a narrow gorge at a good grade IV until easing off before the main road bridge before Abercraf. Egress is on the left GR826127.

NANT TYWYNNI

Map:	Brecon Beacons
Length:	4 Km
Grade:	IV
Access:	A4067 Abercraf to Sennybridge road
Notes	Barbed wire, low bridges and one fall require portaging.

General Introduction

A second tributary of the Tawe this can only be run when in full spate. Entertaining in its own way it is perhaps a worthwhile alternative when the upper Tawe is too high!

TOWER TO CONFLUENCE 4 Km Grade IV

On a very wet day it is possible to launch onto the stream where the main road crosses the river GR867193. The stream is less wide than the length of a boat but is entertaining enough in its own right. Some way down is a steep fall onto rock that is best portaged, especially if using your own boat! Various barbed wires are slung across the river on the section below this drop - these need to be portaged. As the river flattens out a low footbridge requires portaging. It is a relief to see that there is no massive stopper guarding the exit to the A4067 road tunnel as you bash through unable to stop. Continue down to egress at the Glyntawe bridge.

AFON TAWE & NANT TYWYNNI

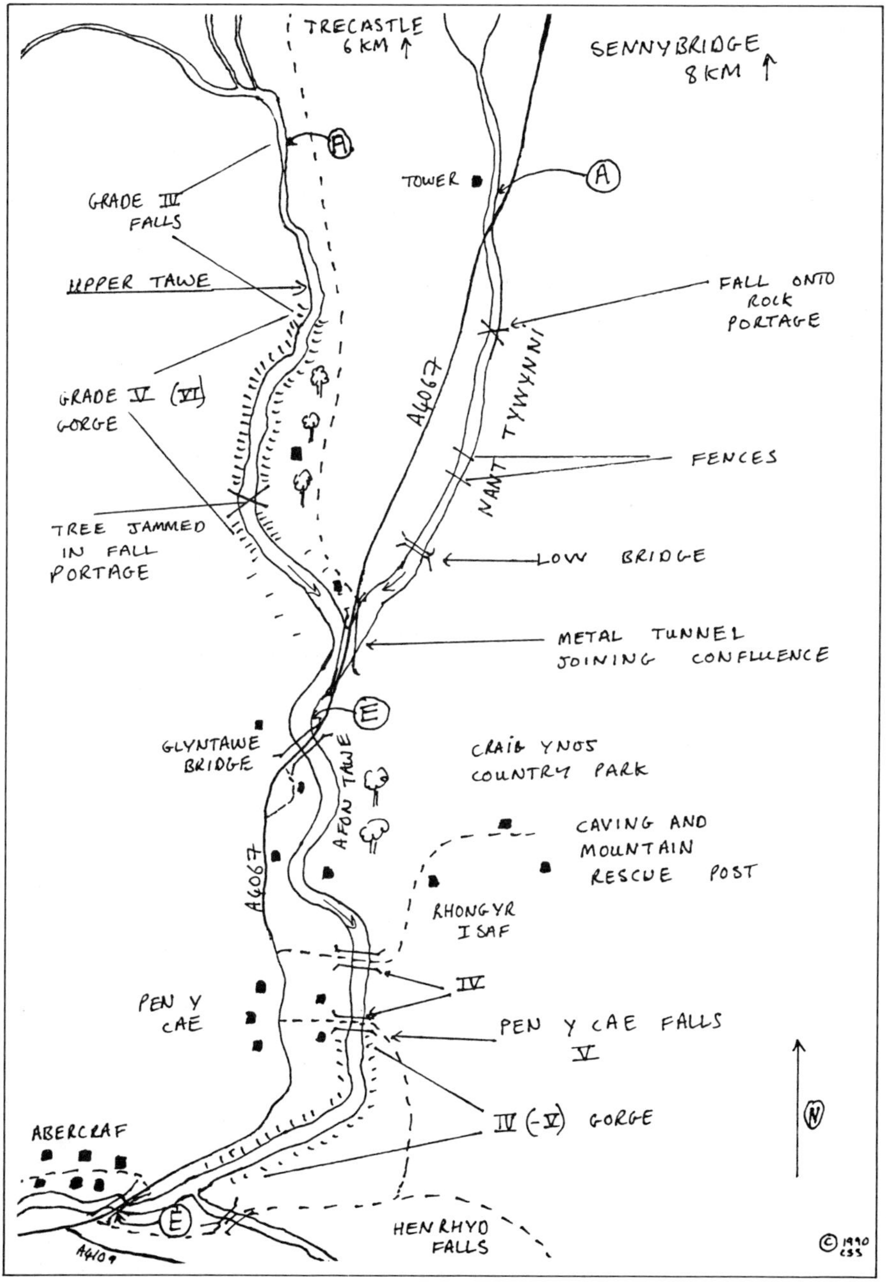

AFON TWRCH

Map: Brecon Beacons No. 160
Length: 5 Km
Grade: IV - V
Access: A4068 Gurnos to Brynamman road
Public House: Tredegar Arms

Notes Two waterfalls need portaging

General Introduction

A bit of an effort is needed to walk in to the top of the Twrch but an excellent albeit serious run is the reward.

PEN YR HELYG TO YSTRADOWEN 5 Km Grade IV - V

Take the small road to Ystradowen off the A4068 down to where the bridge crosses the river at GR755126. If the rapid below the bridge is an easy grade II with most of the rocks covered then you are in for an exciting run. Any higher and the tight gorges become hectic. It is possible to drive up the track on the true left bank (after asking permission from the farms on route!) From the end of the track it is possible to walk up the bank for a kilometre or so and put in below a 20 ft waterfall. This fall is a very dangerous proposition when the rest of the river is up although it has been run when lower.

Below the fall, bouncy rapids take the paddler down to a sharp left hand corner. Just past this is a good rapid with a big stopper at the bottom end. The river narrows as it enters a superb short gorge. This should be inspected before entering. There is one very tight drop at the bottom which is serious and awkward when the river is high. This is grade V at this level.

The river opens out before bending to the right. Inspection is necessary as lurking around one of the corners is a very dangerous grade VI fall. This has been shot but requires just the right level and plenty of protection. A right hand pot hole and an undercut on the left make it a serious proposition. It is best portaged along the slippery ledge on the right.

Below this the river eases off although some narrows near the old quarry workings are of interest. Some sloping weir-like drops above the egress at Ystradowen bridge can provide some entertainment. An excellent run!

YSTRADOWEN TO TAWE CONFLUENCE 7 Km Grade III

I haven't run this section but have had it recommended as worthwhile at a good grade III. There are at least three weirs which may require portaging especially one found beneath one of the bridges. Just before the Tawe confluence is a very large weir that looks particularly unpleasant. Make of this what you will or go back and run the top again.

AFON TWRCH

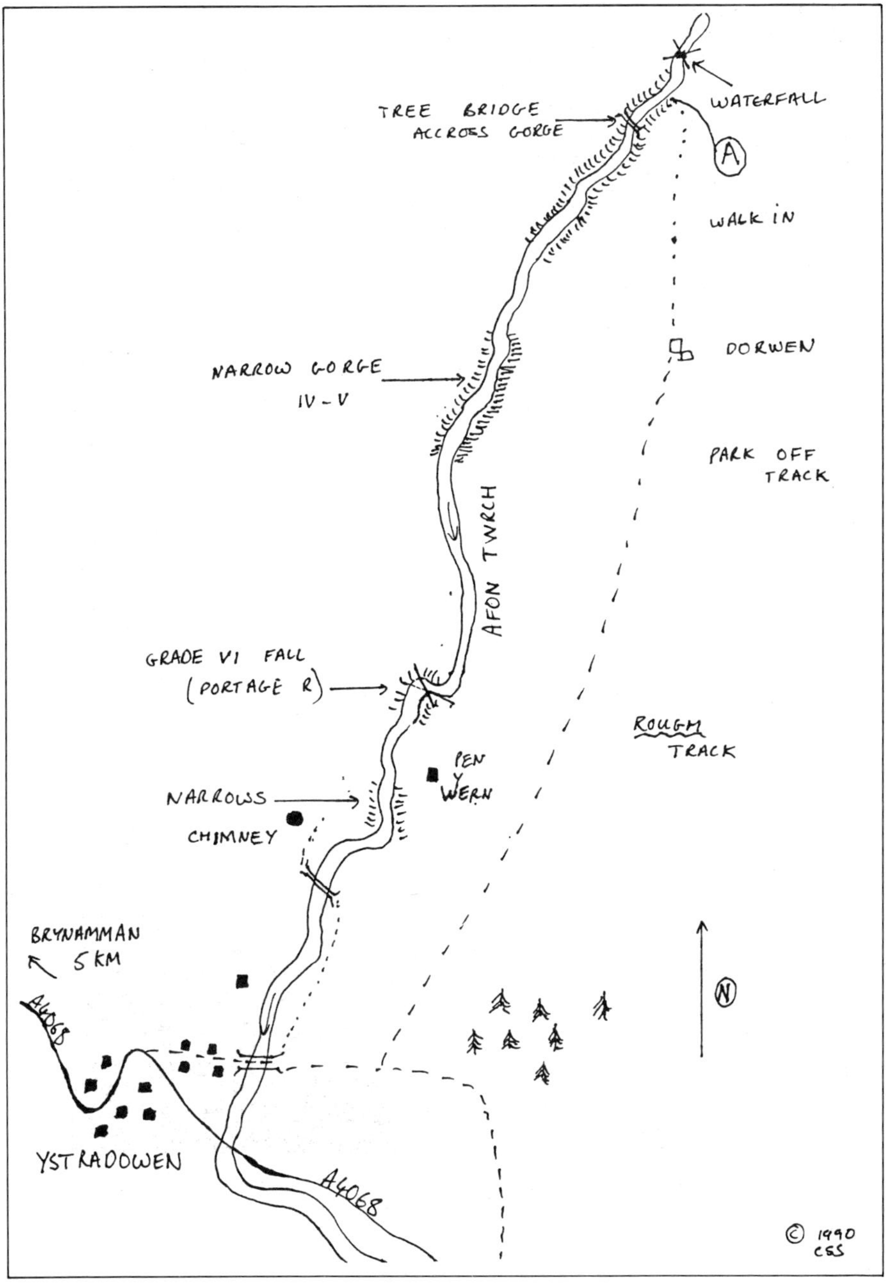
TREE BRIDGE ACCROSS GORGE
WATERFALL
A
WALK IN
DORWEN
NARROW GORGE
IV - V
PARK OFF TRACK
AFON TWRCH
GRADE VI FALL (PORTAGE R)
ROUGH TRACK
PEN Y WERN
NARROWS
CHIMNEY
BRYNAMMAN 5 KM
N
A4068
YSTRADOWEN
A4068
© 1990 CSS

Afon Twrch. Photo: Angelo Conti photo library

AFON SAWDDE

Map: Brecon Beacons No. 160
Length: 9 Km
Grade: III - IV 1 Fall IV - V
Access: A4099 Llangadog to Brynamman road
Public House: The Three Horseshoes GR728245

Notes: One hard fall grade IV - V on the upper river, one fence on upper stretch. The gauge on the egress weir should read 6 - 9 for a good level and grade III in the lower gorge. Any higher and it becomes a continual grade IV with long swim possibilities. There are low wires across the lower stretch.

General Introduction

The Sawdde is a beautiful river containing a lovely gorge on the lower section with many excellent play waves.

LLWYNFRON TO CEFN COED COMMON 9 Km Grade III - IV One Fall IV - V

The access point is fairly awkward to locate and so you are advised to use an O.S. map. Take the small roads up to Twynllanan and turn off right back towards the river. The next on the right leads you down to a small bridge that crosses the river GR757236. At levels greater than 6 on the lower scale there is usually enough water to put on here by the right bank. Trees and one fence are the only problem for about a kilometre or so. The walls then begin to close in and a short gorge waits on a right angled bend. The narrow entrance rapid and following stretch rushing through sculptured red rock are grade IV, or V at very high level. Passing under a green pipe the confluence and main A4069 are reached. The rapids begin to build up and Pont ar Llechau is reached (3 Horse Shoes Pub). An excellent grade III (or IV) gorge follows. Savour this, for it is the very best of the Sawdde.

It is very difficult to pull a swimmer out of this gorge or to know what to do with one when you have. The rock walls are very rounded, making climbing out very difficult. It is best to inspect this section before you run it. At high flows a pipe and wire crossing the river a little way down may need to be portaged. A good egress point is on the right bank just before the measuring weir next to the main A4069 road GR712266. A superb run.

AFON SAWDDE

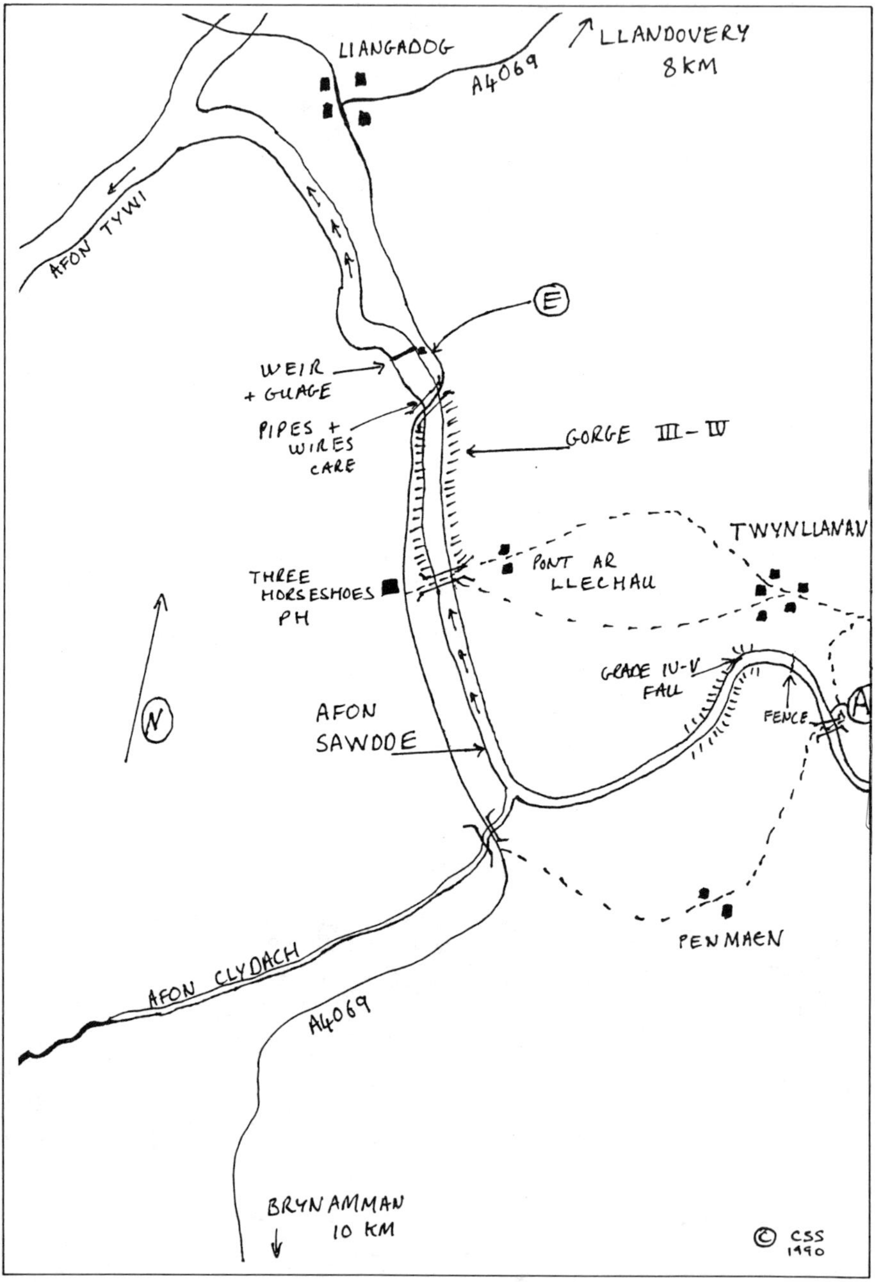
LLANGADOG
LLANDOVERY
8KM
A4069
AFON TYWI
E
WEIR
+ GUAGE
PIPES +
WIRES
CARE
GORGE III – IV
TWYNLLANAN
PONT AR
LLECHAU
THREE
HORSESHOES
PH
GRADE IV-V
FALL
FENCE
N
AFON
SAWDDE
PENMAEN
AFON CLYDACH
A4069
BRYNAMMAN
10 KM
© CSS
1990

AFON GWILI

Maps: Cardigan and surrounding area 145
Lampeter, Llandovery and surrounding area 146
Swansea, Gower and surrounding area 159
Length: 8 Km
Grade: II
Access: A484
Public House: Rock and Fountain

Notes Trees are a problem in high water

General Introduction

A popular river for groups. Local access officer Huw Evans of White Water Consultancy has an access agreement - telephone 0267 237093.

ROCK AND FOUNTAIN TO CARMARTHEN 8 Km Grade II

Access is by the friendly Welsh pub the Rock and Fountain on the main A484 Carmarthen road GR389258. It is best run after rain when good playwaves are plentiful. There is one small weir a little way down the run which is safe to play in.

One drop a few miles on reaches grade III and is excellent for playing on. Egress by the A484 road bridge river right remembering to shut the gate!

AFON TYWI

Map: Swansea, Gower and surrounding area No. 159
Length: 19 Km
Grade: Touring
Access: A485 Carmarthen to Lampeter road

General Information

An excellent touring stretch.

A485 ROAD BRIDGE TO LLANSTEPHAN BOAT HOUSE

Start the run on the Gwili from the A485 road bridge GR431219 (alternatively you may start from the quayside in Carmarthen itself). The river meanders through pleasant countryside with the odd ripply rapid here and there. The river is excellent for estuarine bird life. It is best to try and coincide paddling the last five or so km when the tide is high. As the tide turns it will quicken your speed tremendously but still allow egress on the right bank by Llanstephan Boating House GR362113. However, take care not to shoot out to sea! At low water you will have to wallow through the mud banks to get off.

AFON GWILI & AFON TYWI

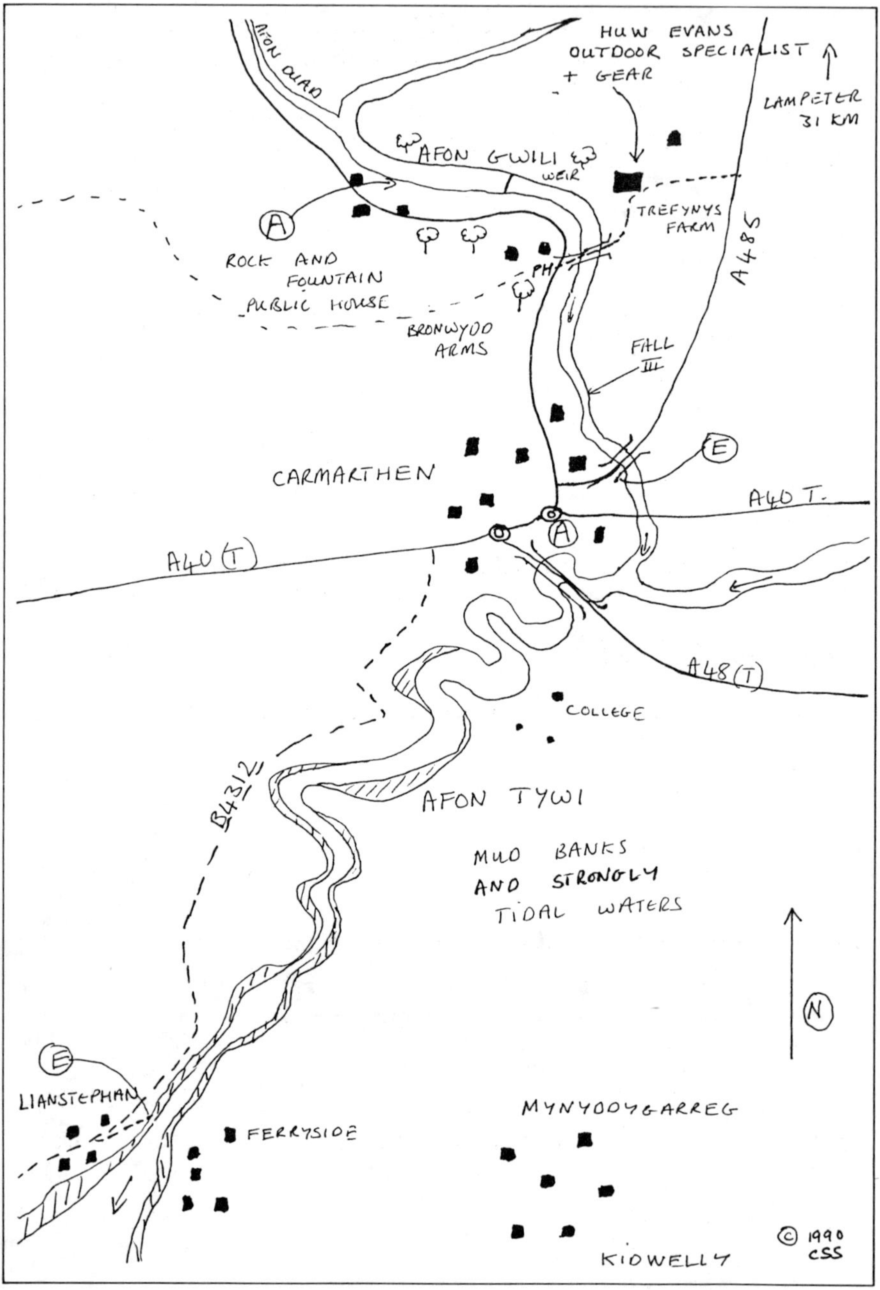

Views of the Gwili. Photo: Angelo Conti photo library

AFON TEIFI - notes only

I haven't paddled the Teifi for years now although there are some good short sections on it. Slaloms are often run at Llandysul where there is an open agreement. The rapids are grade II - III with some excellent waves in time of flood. Ring local access officer for details of this agreement.

There are also notable falls at the villages of Henllan and Cenarth. At Newcastle Emlyn are some stepped weirs good for playing in at lower water levels. These form horrendous stoppers during time of flood.

Cenarth Falls. Photo: Angelo Conti photo library

AFON COTHI

Map: Lampeter, Llandovery and surrounding area No. 146
Swansea, Gower and surrounding area No. 159
Length: 35 Km
Grade: II - III
Access: A482 Llanwrda to Lampeter road

Notes Trees are a problem. One in particular on the Abergorlech gorge is locally known for catching boats lost upstream.

General Introduction

An excellent touring river through pleasant surroundings with the odd surprise in store. Unusual in having no man made weirs.

BRYNTEG TO TYWI CONFLUENCE 35 Km Grade II - III

Take the small right hand turn off the A482 coming from Llanwrdu just before crossing the river at Pumsaint. Follow this to the bridge at Brynteg, GR684433, where access may be had from the footpath on the right bank. The river needs to be fairly high to make the run worthwhile. A wire slung low and fallen trees need some careful negotiating but they are fairly obvious. A short distance on and you may be surprised (especially so in flood) to see vehicles driving through the river. This is only the Landre fording point.

The Pumsaint bridge (A482) has barbed wire slung from it and needs caution in high water. Tributaries swell the river but make it no harder than the odd grade II as it flows towards Abergorlech. As the banks close in and significant forestation occurs the Abergorlech gorge is approached. This is similar in formation to the Sawdde gorge in as much as the rounded rocks make access and egress slippery. When a drop looking slightly larger than anything before is reached it is wise to get out on the right hand footpath and inspect the next few hundred metres or so. At the time of writing a tree choke blocked the whole river requiring a difficult portage! This is well known locally! The river opens out before the banks close in again after the bridge at Ynysowen. There are some good playspots and swirls here. Egress is best river right by the B4310 road bridge just after the confluence with the Tywi GR493203.

AFON COTHI

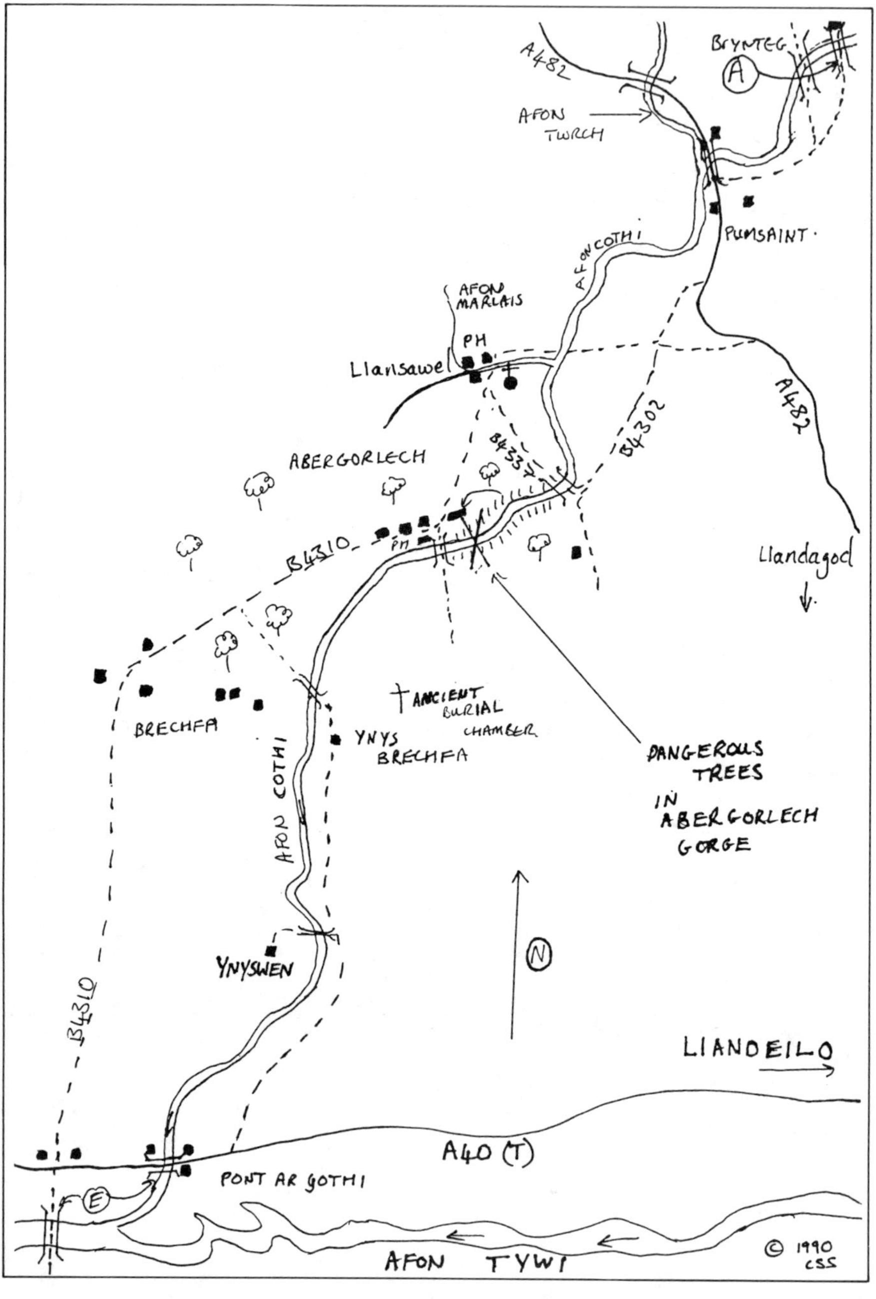
A482
BRYNTEG
A
AFON
TWRCH
PUMSAINT
AFON COTHI
AFON
MARLAIS
PH
Llansawel
A482
B4302
B4337
ABERGORLECH
B4310
PH
Llandagod
ANCIENT
BURIAL
CHAMBER
YNYS
BRECHFA
BRECHFA
AFON COTHI
DANGEROUS
TREES
IN
ABERGORLECH
GORGE
N
YNYSWEN
B4310
LLANDEILO
A40 (T)
PONT AR GOTHI
E
AFON TYWI
© 1990
CSS

RIVER USK

Map: Brecon Beacons No. 160
Abergavenny and the Black Mountains No. 161
Cardiff, Newport and surrounding area No. 171
Length: 104 Km
Grade: Sections of I, II, III (IV in spate).
Access: Various points. There is an ongoing access agreement on the Usk. Extra permission is required to canoe through the Glanusk estate. This is partially for the paddlers own good so as not to be peppered by shotgun pellets from the regular shoots held here. Seek advice from the access officer, W.C.A.

Notes In high water several of the natural weir steps can produce dangerous stoppers and towbacks. If in doubt portage.

General Introduction

Along with the Wye the Usk is one of the most popular rivers in South Wales. It has sections to please most paddlers from bouncy upper rapids and beautiful lower touring stretches. It descends from the northern foothills of the Black Mountain range. Interestingly enough, when full to the brim, it normally shows a wild red colour derived from the sandstone beds that its numerous tributaries flow from.

PANTYSGALLOG TO BRECON 19 Km Grade II - III (Map No. 160)

Passing westwards on the A40(T) 4 km from Sennybridge there is a small road on the left which crosses the river GR904292. Just above is a four foot drop that can be shot (with care in high water). The river bubbles gently at grade II through pleasantly wooded banks towards Sennybridge. There is alternate access on the small road to the Sennybridge training camp GR919286. There are three main natural weir drops on this section. The first on a right hand bend, is fairly straight forward, although trees on the far right can be a problem. The second, a short distance after, needs to be inspected in high water as it forms a big stopper. The third and biggest drop is a little way on after some easy rapids. In spate, it forms a dangerous towback in its Horseshoe shaped left hand side. Portage if in doubt.

Grade II - III rapids take the paddler down to Brecon. Even in low water there is a superb play stopper on one of these. Egress may be made at the Aberbran bridge GR987292. The farmer is quite amenable when asked for permission. Better still is easy egress on the left hand bank into a car park on the outskirts of Brecon GR038289.

BRECON TO TALYBONT

Maps: No. 160,161
Length: 14 Km
Grade: II
Access: by the car-park (as above egress)
Public House: The Star Inn, Talybont on Usk

This excellent, gentle section is popular for beginners' groups and S.I. assessments! There is a shoot on the left of the large sloping weir in Brecon which saves scraping over elsewhere. Trees on bends are the only problems as the canoeist winds down gentle rapids, the Brecon Beacons overlooking from the right. There is a small broken weir, a little way beneath the aqueduct carrying the Monmouthshire and Brecon canal. The river eases off more and meanders its way through gentle farmland. Egress is at the Llansantfffraed to Talybont on Usk road bridge, reached by turning off the A40(T) road GR123233. Details of the access agreement may be seen here on the right.

Fun on the Usk. Photo: Angelo Conti photo library

RIVER USK - sections 1 & 2

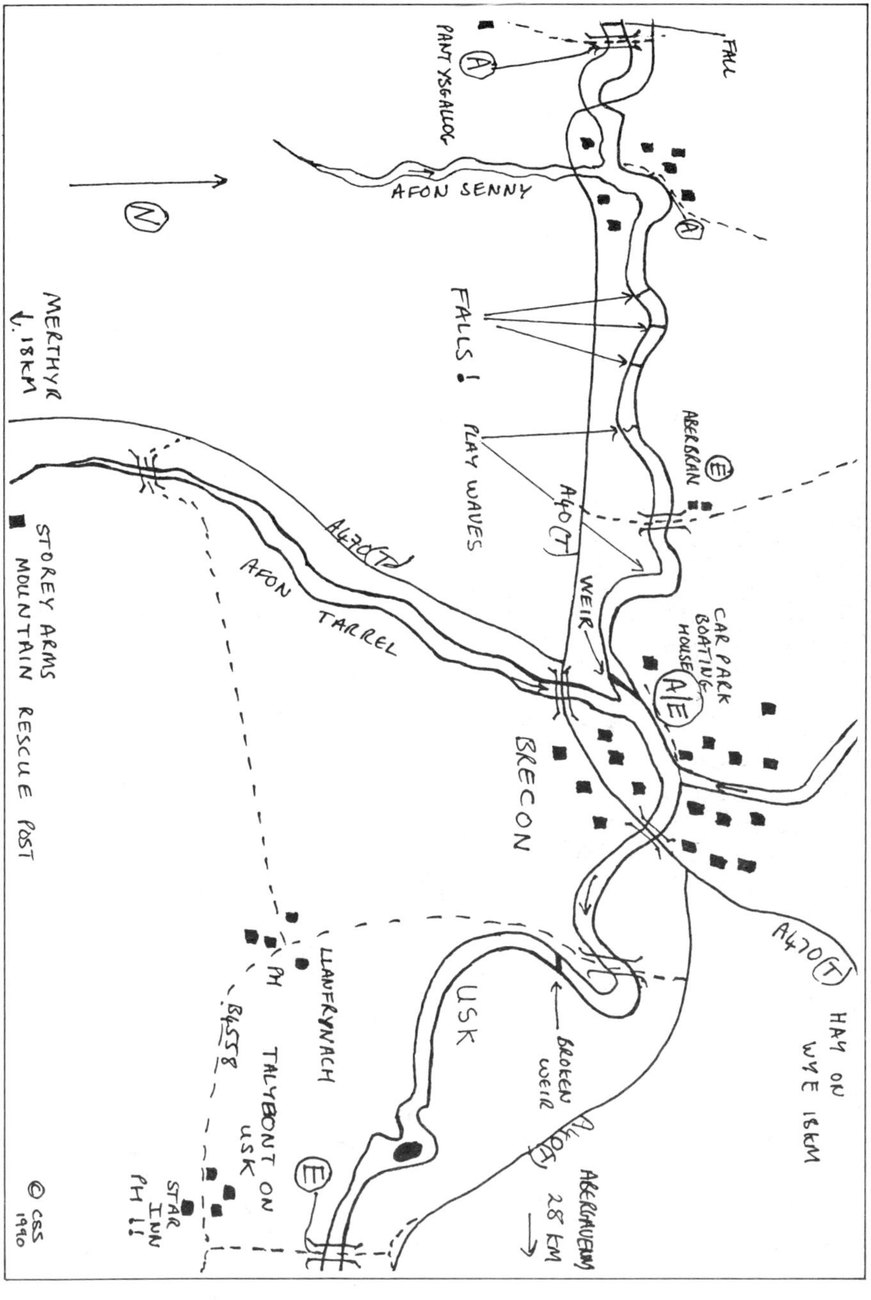

TALYBONT ON USK TO LLANGYNIDR 7 Km Grade III (IV)

When full to the brim this section rages down usually with a brick red hue to it. It stays up after other rivers have dropped and as such is excellent at the grade.

Grade I-II rapids lead in to the Mill falls, which begin soon after a church on the right bank. The falls are probably best run right to left to avoid a large stopper on the right half way down. In very high water these falls may reach grade IV. In low water a series of steps and pools exist. Bouncy water leads the paddler down to Llangynidr bridge where egress can be made (GR152203) on the left hand banks. Parking has to be up in the village and the people are friendly so don't upset them please!

LLANGYNIDR BRIDGE TO CRICKHOWELL 11 Km Grade III (IV) (Map No. 161)

Below the bridge there is a ledge which in high water forms a boat and person gobbling stopper from which many pub stories have originated. This is best avoided. A little way further is the so called Spuhler's folly ledge. This is best inspected, for at higher water levels it can form a dangerous stopper. Portage if in doubt. This is the best of the river from the white water paddler's eyes. Egress is about a half km below Crickhowell on the right hand bank where a suitable lay-by is found (A4077) GR218178.

One of the Usk's many steps. Photo: Angelo Conti photo library

RIVER USK - sections 3 & 4

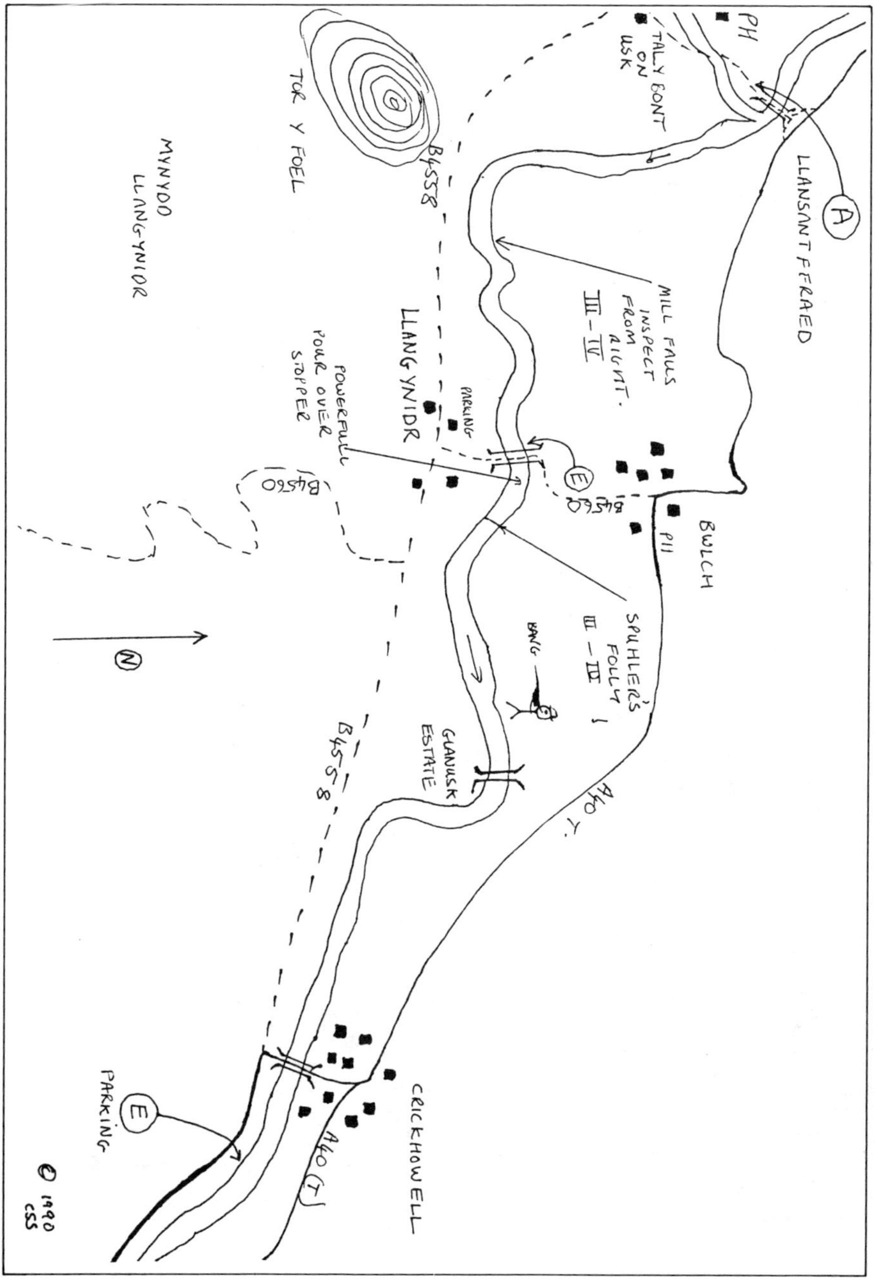

CRICKHOWELL TO CAERLEON 75 Km Grade I - II (Map No. 161 and 171)

An excellent section for those who enjoy touring the gentler river. Scramble down the steep right bank (egress for the previous section) at GR218178. Trees are the only real problem on a river like this especially where they hang over bends. The rapids never reach more than grade II and decrease in frequency on route to Caerleon. Passing the Sugar Loaf on the left, Abergavenny is reached where there is a small broken weir directly below the main road bridge. The easiest route is the right arch. If time permits the castle and museum on the left are well worth a visit. Some way after Abergavenny footpaths of the pretty Usk Valley walk run alongside the river. Where the B4598 comes close to the river some 6 km short of Usk is a boxed-in small weir. This is obvious from the river with the weir buildings river left. The stopper is quite fierce at high flows but at normal levels is no problem providing the canoe punches straight through without being caught sideways! Portage if in any doubt. A few broken steps take the paddler to Usk. The grassy banks by the main road bridge in Usk provide an alternative egress thus saving 20 odd kms to Caerleon. Usk is a beautiful small town full of pleasant watering establishments and is well worth a stop anyway.

The next stop is at the small roadbridge at Newbridge on Usk GR385948. Egress is a bit scrambly up the left bank but the Newbridge Inn is very friendly and a beer is good at this stage. The remaining section to Caerleon is tidal and is hard work if a big tide is on the flood. However, if you can time high water slack or just after it is possible to egress river left at the B4236 bridge and straight into the Ship Inn GR342903. Low water is best avoided although the trudge up the steep mud bank isn't too grim.

Playing the Usk. Photo: Angelo Conti photo library

RIVER USK - section 5

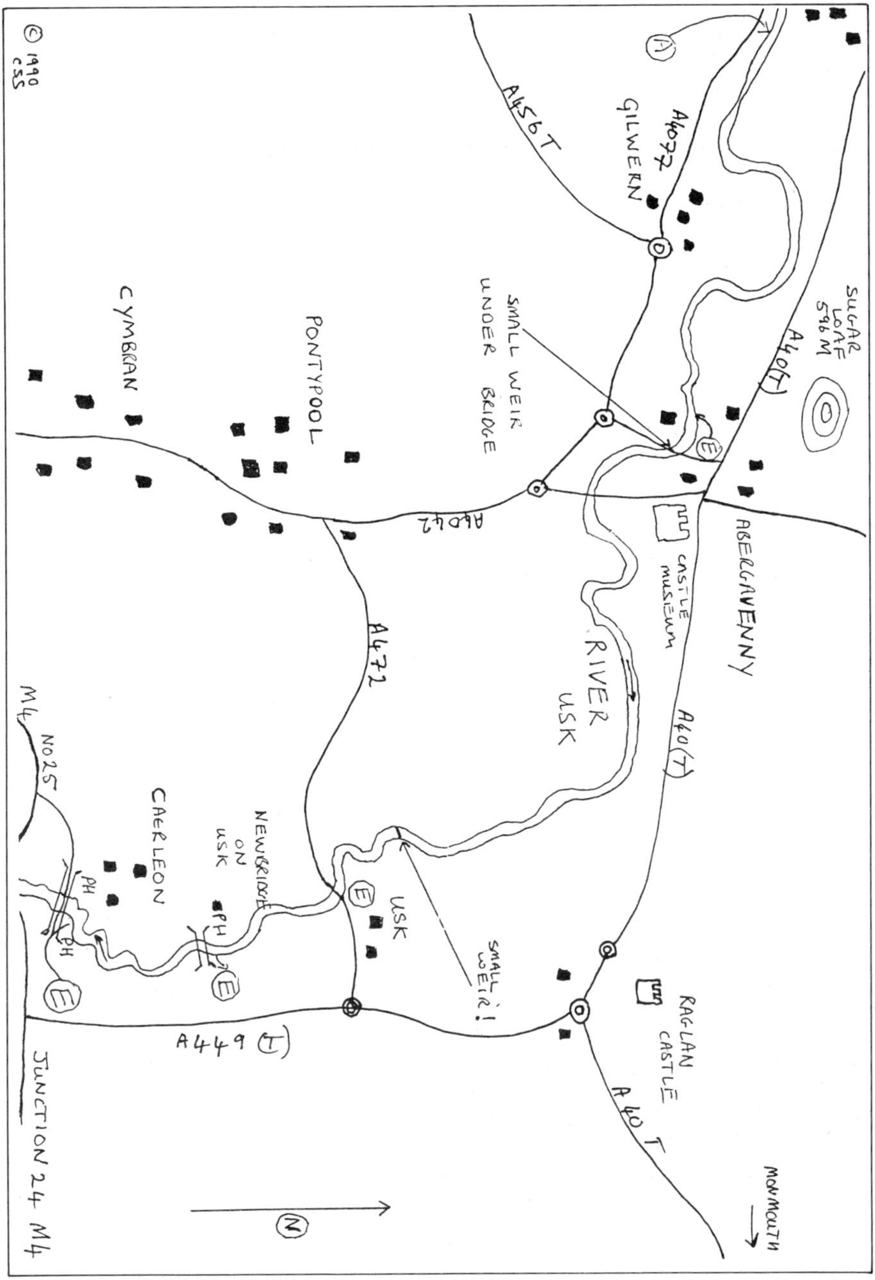

AFON RHYMNEY

Maps: Abergavenny and the Black Mountains No. 161
Cardiff, Newport and surround areas No. 171
Length: 54 Km
Grade: Section of III (IV) and I - II
Access: A489 Caerphilly to Pontlottyn road

Notes One weir needs to be portaged, as does one tunnel.

General Introduction

The upper Rhymney is an exciting paddle at high water. There are quite a few hazards, which from personal experience require and deserve respect. A serious undertaking at the grade!

PONTLOTTYN TO LLANBRADACH 24 Km Grade II - III (IV)

The river needs to be in spate to run from Pontlottyn. Put on by the bridge below where the river comes spurting angrily out from the confines of a tunnel GR117063. Bounce down on fast grade II - III water. The only problem being low fences which require care. Craggy outcrops are passed on the left and some few kilometres further on the river passes down a dark tunnel. This must be portaged on the right 100 metres before. The river is fast but easy here although not a place for beginners. An excellent section of rapids follows.

As the river approaches Bargoed extreme care must be taken due to a dangerous weir on a boxed-in section of the river. This should be inspected beforehand. Turn off the main A469 down the steep road to Gilfach railway station GR153992. A steep track goes off left, crossing the river and giving access to a power station-like building. Park here and walk 600 m upstream, where the weir can be seen above a bridge and boxed-in between 30 ft sheer brick walls. You must break out 400 metres or so above where it is possible to climb out up crumbly banks. This is just below another bridge - not a place to swim. In high water I have seen large objects recirculate from 20 ft. downstream - ooh horrible!

The easiest place to put on is above the power station. The rapids flow under some large concrete slabs crossing the river. The next few hundred metres are grade III - IV. A pipe under the road bridge requires care. There is another broken weir a kilometre or so down stream which can be shot. Below this is an excellent mini gorge through which the water swirls at grade II - III. One more fall at the bottom of the gorge reaches III (just below a small road bridge). After an impressive viaduct the water eases off with weirs being the only problem. At high water spate the ones by the egress in Llanbradach form powerful stoppers and towbacks. At lower water these look totally innocuous. Portage left or right if in doubt.

Egress by these weirs onto the estate roads which are right next to the river GR155915.

AFON RHYMNEY - section 1

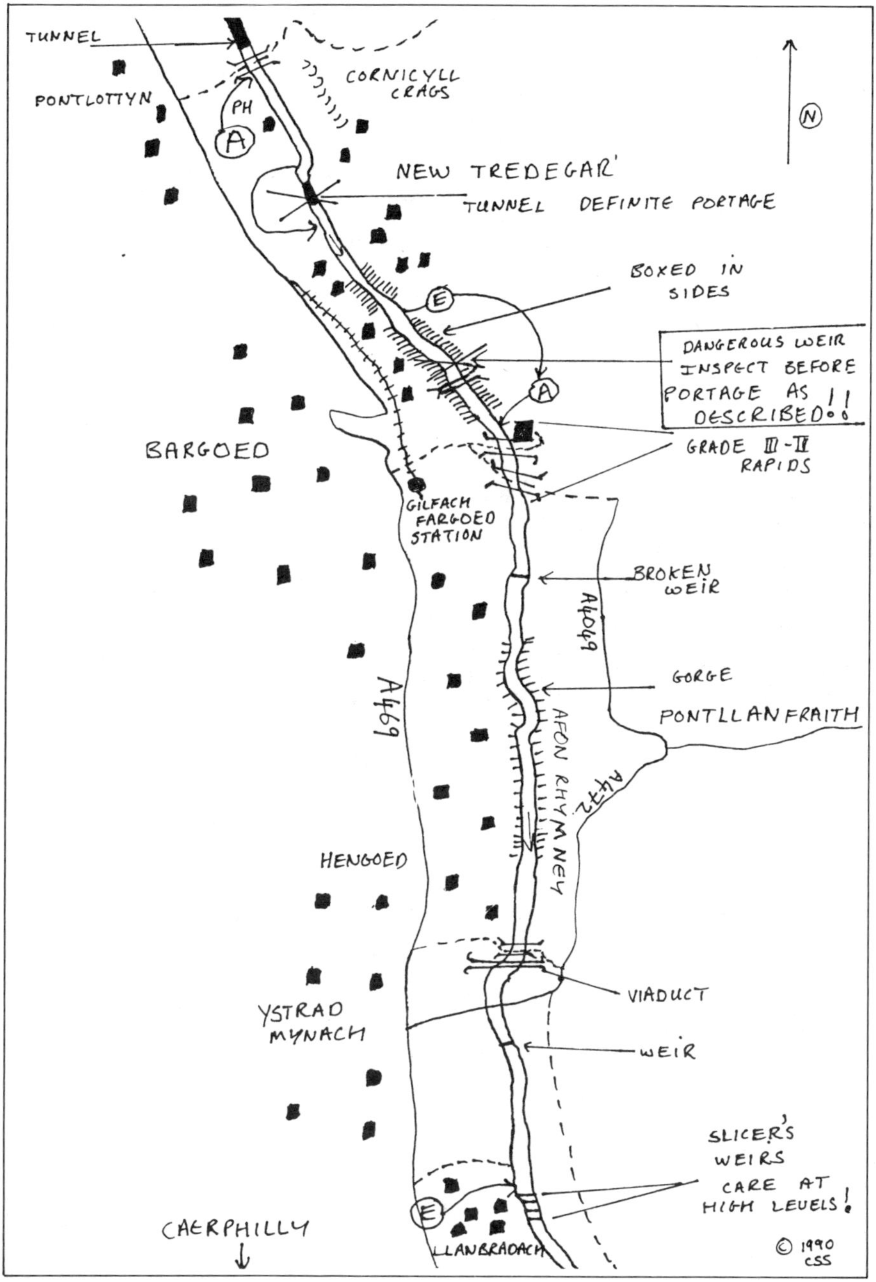

LLANBRADACH TO CARDIFF 30 Km Grade II

A pleasant paddle as the seriousness of the upper section relaxes on its way to the sea. Access is below the Llanbradach weirs which were described above. Trees are the only problem on the first section. At off flood conditions an excellent beginners surfing wave can be found a little way down. A few km on, an obvious weir needs to be inspected. This is between Bedwas and Machen. If in doubt portage. The river meanders as it follows the attractive Rhymney valley footpath walk. There are several bridges on route that make easy egress points for those not wishing to go the full way to Cardiff. Under one small bridge before the M4 motorway crossing an entertaining stopper waits on the right hand arch! Just before the A48 bridge is a measuring weir with a tree in the left hand side. Another is found 3 km further on in Llanrumney. Both form boxed-in stoppers especially in high water. Egress at one of the many road bridges towards the Estuary.

Surfing a small wave. Photo: Angelo Conti photo library

AFON RHYMNEY - section 2

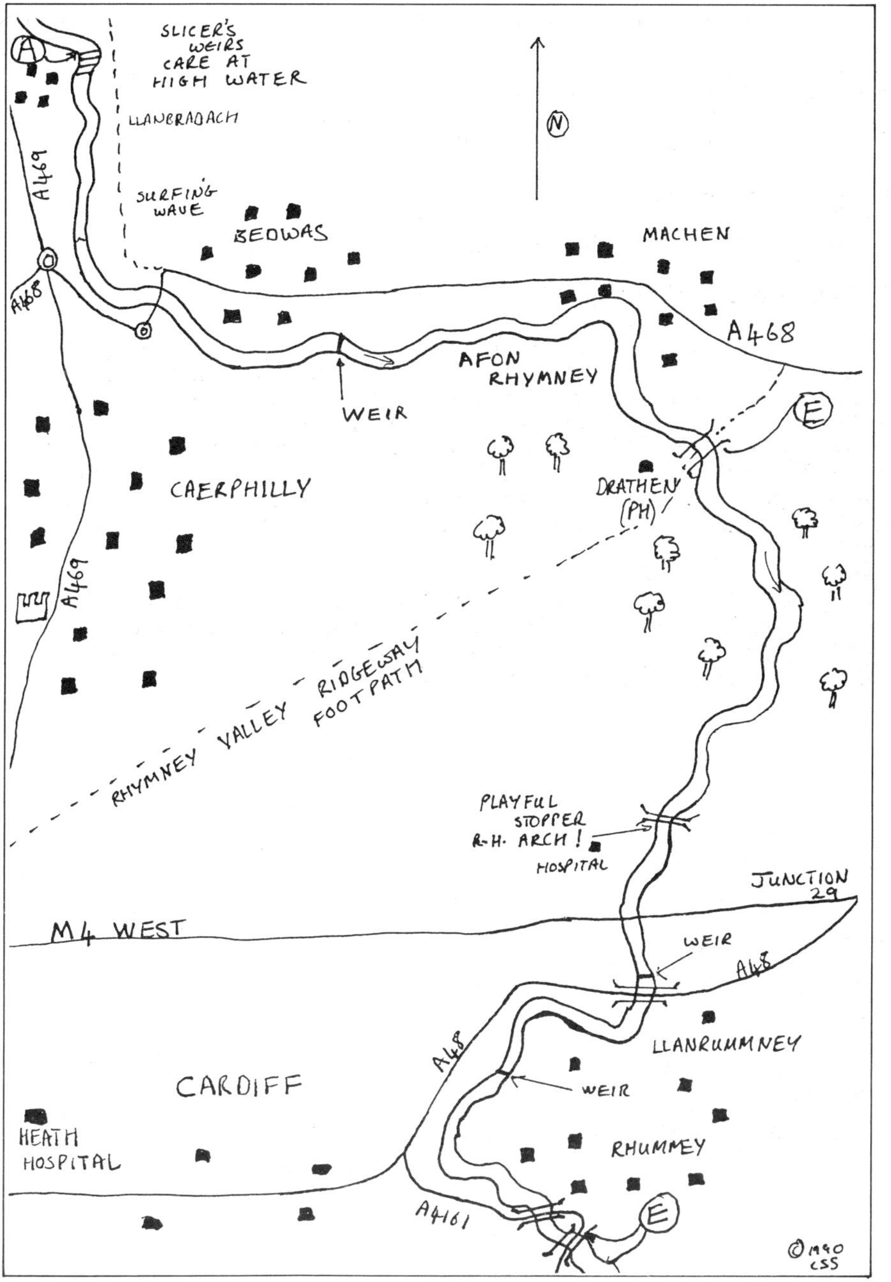

AFON EBBW

Map: Cardiff and Newport and surrounding areas No. 171
Length: 17 Km
Grade: II
Access: Risca to Newbridge road A467

Notes Weirs may require respect. Low wires!

General Introduction

A pleasant easy area excellent for training.

CWMCARN TO NEWPORT 17 Km Grade II

Access is best made above the Sirhowy confluence by a small bridge that crosses the river in Cwmcarn GR216937. Two small weir steps occur soon after the start. Easy but interesting water is doubled in volume with the Sirhowy entering from the right. By a sports ground with obvious floodlights, care should be taken as low wires cross the river. These may be covered in high water! There are 2 weirs just before and after the power station (on river left). Both can produce strong stoppers in times of flood and the second although small is boxed-in. If in any doubt portage left or right.

There is one more weir just before the main road bridge in Bassaleg. It is a large sloping affair broken down in recent floods especially on the left. Inspect to assess stopper and debris. Portage over the road if necessary. Egress by the road bridge at Maes Glas GR298857.

AFON EBBW

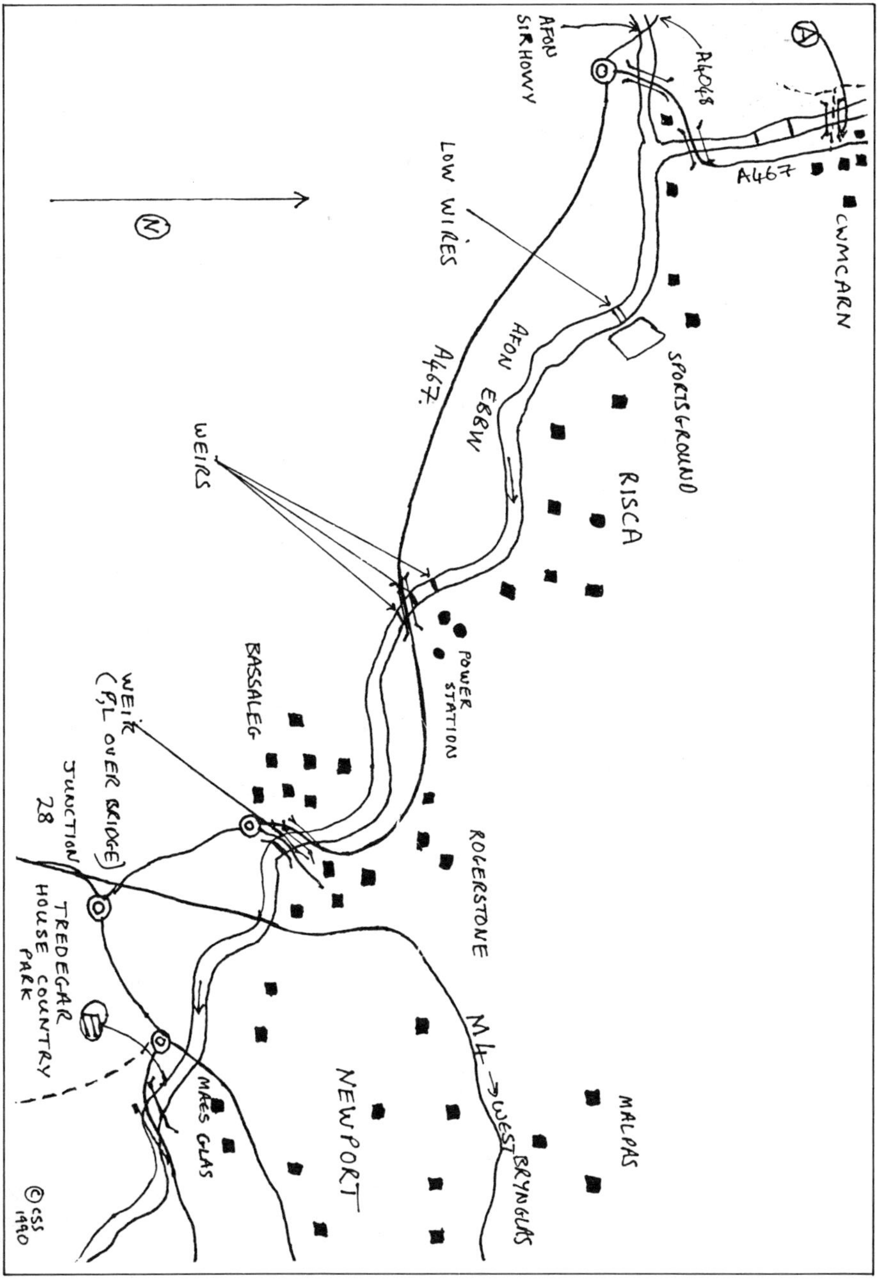
A
AFON SIRHOWY
A4048
A467
CWMCARN
LOW WIRES
N
AFON EBBW
A467.
SPORTS GROUND
RISCA
WEIRS
POWER STATION
BASSALEG
WEIR (P/L OVER BRIDGE)
JUNCTION 28
ROGERSTONE
TREDEGAR HOUSE COUNTRY PARK
E
M4 → WEST
MAES GLAS
NEWPORT
MALPAS
BRYNGLAS
© CSS 1990

AFON LWYD

Map: Cardiff and Newport and surrounding area No. 171
Length: 18 Km
Grade: II
Access: Newport to Pontypool road A4042(T)
Public House: Ship Inn at egress point

Notes Trees to be portaged, one weir needs respect in high water.

General Introduction

An easy but quite attractive river teeming with animal and bird life. Ends in tidal stretch.

PONTYPOOL TO CAERLEON 18 Km Grade II

A good access point is from waste ground by a small road and bridge leading into the village of New Inn GR298995. The river is best paddled after reasonable rainfall when the canoe will float down the shingle rapids. This is a pleasant run although nowhere reaching greater than grade II. Trees require portaging depending on recent storm damage but this is a pleasant paddle finishing up as it does in estuarine water. There are two easy small weirs in Llanyrafon. The first produces a surprisingly strong stopper in times of high water: The greatest danger on this part of the river is being hit by golf balls from the course on the left. However, the golfers and for that matter the fishermen seem extremely friendly here!

There is one weir in between the railway and road bridges in Ponthir that requires caution. It consists of 3 boxed-in sections the middle one of which is best avoided. The left is OK (although boxed) at normal river flow. A good egress point is after the Lwyd joins the Usk (described elsewhere in this book). The bridge at Caerleon is suitable with a pub each side. This section is strongly tidal and you may therefore wish to time your runs. GR342903.

AFON LWYD

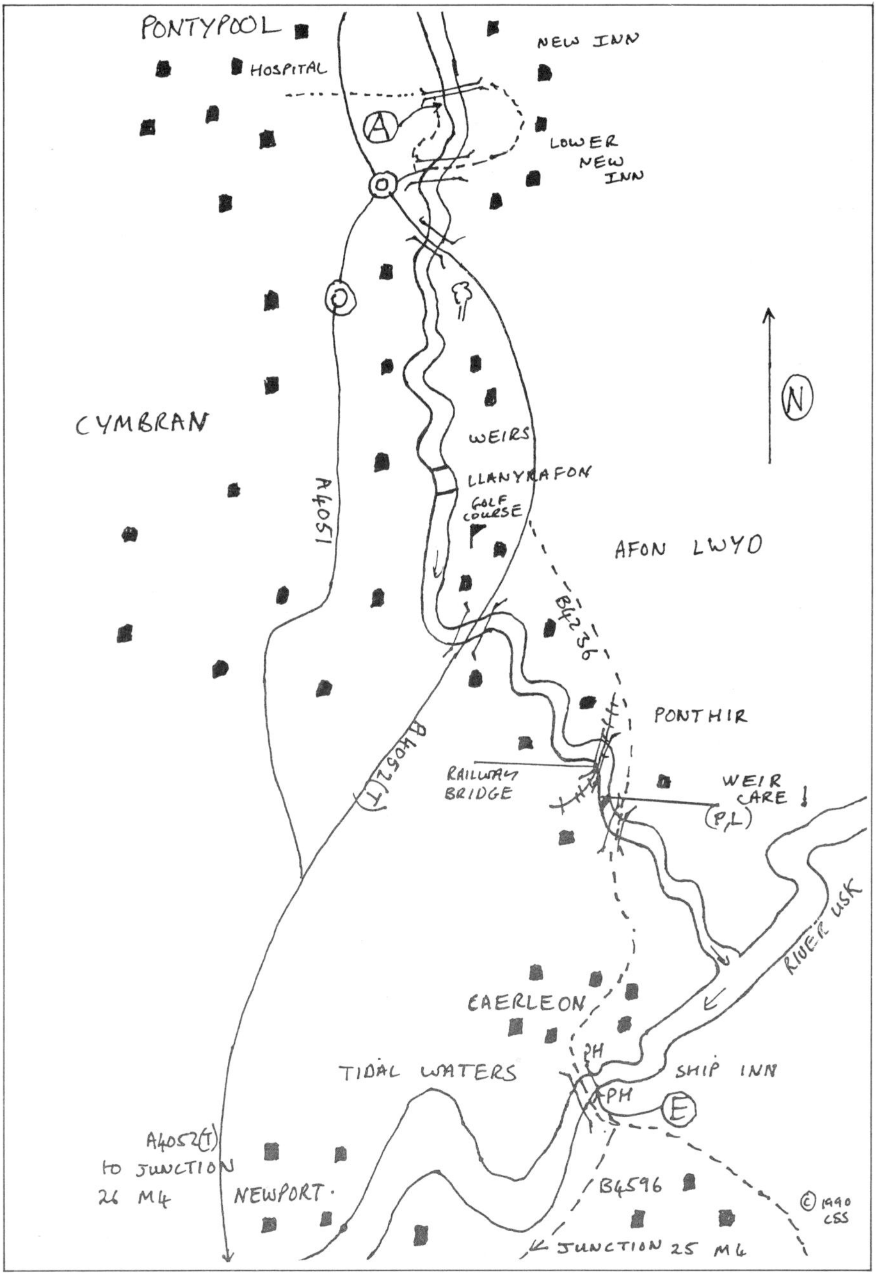
PONTYPOOL
NEW INN
HOSPITAL
A
LOWER NEW INN
N
CYMBRAN
WEIRS
LLANYRAFON
GOLF COURSE
A4051
AFON LWYD
B4236
PONTHIR
A4052(T)
RAILWAY BRIDGE
WEIR CARE !
(P,L)
RIVER USK
CAERLEON
PH
TIDAL WATERS
SHIP INN
PH
E
A4052(T) to JUNCTION 26 M4
NEWPORT
B4596
© 1990 CSS
JUNCTION 25 M4

notes

notes

notes

notes

notes